The Sto
of a Tre~~~

Claudia Orange

BWB

BRIDGET WILLIAMS BOOKS

First published in 1989 by Allen & Unwin New Zealand Limited in association with
the Port Nicholson Press, Private Bag, Wellington, New Zealand.
Reprinted 1989, 1990 (March, July)

Reprinted in 1992, 1993, 1994, 1996, 1997, 2000 (twice), 2001, 2002, 2004 and 2005
by Bridget Williams Books Limited, P. O. Box 5482, Wellington, New Zealand

ISBN 0 04 641053 8

The following photographs and illustrations, indicated by page number, are
reproduced by courtesy of:
Alexander Turnbull Library, pp. 3, 4 (bottom), 6, 8 (bottom), 9 10, 12, 13, 21,
    24, 27 (bottom), 32, 36, 38, 39 (J. K. Hall collection), 40, 41, 44, 46, 47
    (Nicholl Album VII, top; Ruck Album V, bottom), 48, 51 (left), 52, 53
    (Urquhart collection), 55, 57, 60, 61, 62, 64 (Burton Brothers collection), 65,
    66 (bottom), 67, 69, 70 (top), 71, 72, 73
Ans Westra, p. 76 (left)
Auckland City Art Gallery, Partridge collection, pp. 19, 28, 45 (right)
Auckland Institute and Museum, pp. 7, 14, 16, 25
Auckland Public Library, pp. 49, 66 (top)
British Library, p. 4 (top)
Canterbury Museum, A. C. Barker collection, p. 51 (right)
Christchurch Press, p. 80
Fiona Clark, p.59
Gil Hanly, p.77 (bottom)
Hawkes Bay Museum, Napier, p. 21 (left)
Hocken Library, Dunedin, p. 29
Marlborough Express, p. 79
National Archives, title page, p. 27 (top)
National Museum of New Zealand, pp. 54, 63, 70 (left)
New Zealand Herald, pp. 75, 78
Northern Advocate, p. 76 (right)
Private collection W. S. Busby, Alexander Turnbull Library, p. 11
Ray Pigney, *Auckland Star*, p. 77 (top)
Rex Nan Kivell Collection, National Library of Australia, p. 8 (top)

The author gratefully acknowledges the assistance of Michael Keith, Mary Louise
Ormsby, Terence Taylor, the 1990 Commission and the staff of the *Dictionary of New Zealand Biography*.

Design by Terence Taylor
Cover design by Lindsay Missen
Typeset by Saba Graphics, Christchurch

Printed by Astra Print, Wellington

Contents

An Independent New Zealand

The Maori people and Cook

The story of the treaty begins in 1769, when the British explorer James Cook first visited the country which Europeans called New Zealand. Cook found a land of independent tribes who thought of themselves as tangata maori – the ordinary people. For them, the arrival of the British meant the beginning of new relationships within New Zealand, as well as with the world beyond.

Maori* and British rapidly established a barter trade. Cook's vessels needed food and water. The Maori were attracted by household items like scissors and mirrors, and by nails (which could be used for carving) and tapa cloth. Each side had to come to terms with the other to get what it wanted. Both sides tried force, but both found more could be gained by friendly relations. It was the beginning of a partnership.

Partnership in trade

In 1788, the British established a convict colony in New South Wales. Sydney soon became the staging post for traders who wanted to exploit New Zealand's resources – particularly seals, whales, timber, and flax. Europeans were usually dependent on Maori for access to these resources, and Maori also supplied provisions and services in return for European goods. By the 1830s many tribes were engaged in trade themselves, cultivating and preparing flax, and producing crops such as potatoes and fruit, and pigs.

Most Europeans who came were temporary visitors. A few, such as missionaries and traders, became more or less permanent. The traders dealt in flax, timber, and general goods. They often built their own trading vessels. The Maori

5

Thoms's whaling station at Porirua near Wellington. By 1839 there were about thirty stations round the coastline of the South Island and the lower part of the North Island. They were often sizeable settlements with European and Maori workers. In the 1830s Maori formed the core of many of the gangs, working the boats and processing the whales.

Changes to Maori communities

The coming of sealers, whalers, and traders brought changes to Maori communities. But one constant concern for Maori leaders remained – war. Traditional reasons for war – such as taking revenge for affronts – continued, but the struggle grew fiercer with guns and as the competition for raw materials increased. From about 1814 northern Maori began to use trade to arm themselves with muskets, powder, and shot. This turned into an arms race and by 1830 all tribes were fully armed.

From 1820 to 1835 wars and migrations caused a major re-distribution of the Maori population. Some say they were also a major cause of population decline. Some say, too, that the changes, the wars, and the loss of life made the Maori people willing to listen to the missionaries. Many Maori leaders were tired of fighting and turned to the missionaries as peacemakers.

people were part of this trade growth, supplying provisions and labour for the business ventures, and also areas of land for the traders to use as a base. The traders' livelihood depended on being on good terms with local Maori.

But by the late 1830s more Europeans saw New Zealand as a place where they could come and live permanently. Sydney men who traded in land began 'buying up' vast areas of Maori land. Such people were not as careful as earlier settlers in their dealings with the Maori. The dependence of Maori and European on each other, a feature of the early years, started to break down, and Maori leaders had a forewarning of the Pakeha drive to seize the land.

The Maori people and the British Crown

The governors (the British Crown's representatives) in New South Wales took a special interest in New Zealand. Governor Phillip King started this. He sent gifts – iron tools, fruit tree seedlings, and livestock – to Te Pahi, a leading chief who controlled a good anchorage for shipping in the Bay of Islands.

Henry and Marianne Williams's 'comfortable home' at the mission at Paihia. From 1823, with the help of other men and women, they preached Christianity there and taught 'useful arts' including reading and writing.

Maori seafarers

Whaling and trading ships often recruited Maori as crew. They 'learnt the ropes' quickly and served on ships of all nationalities. Many travelled to Australia, Asia, North America, England, and Europe. Some spent up to three and four years on the ships. But there were many cases of Maori being ill-treated on board, and of their being taken on in New Zealand and then abandoned in Sydney and elsewhere and cheated of their wages.

Governor King invited a Maori group in Sydney to discuss these matters with him, but, because New Zealand was beyond British rule of law, there was nothing he or other governors could to do stop such things happening.

Te Pahi and several of his sons visited New South Wales in 1805 and presented King with fine cloaks and a stone mere. King invited them to stay at Government House – and they did, for nearly three months. King was impressed by Te Pahi's ability and shrewdness; his relationship with Te Pahi convinced him that Maori and British could work together.

Meanwhile the New South Wales chaplain Samuel Marsden began to take a particular interest in Maori visitors. He wanted Maori to become interested in Christianity; and so he invited chiefs and their sons to visit him at his Parramatta home. There they learned agricultural techniques and trade skills.

Sydney, 1823, the major centre for trade in the South Pacific. Maori sailors were a common sight both here and in Hobart in the 1820s and 1830s.

By 1836 Kororareka (Russell) had become a busy port of call for Sydney traders and British, French, American, and colonial whalers. Chiefs and their people from a wide surrounding area traded provisions and services in exchange for European goods.

Titore, an important chief of the Bay of Islands. In January 1835, one of the King of England's secretaries wrote to 'His Highness Titore': 'Friend and Brother, I have received the commands of my most gracious sovereign King William the Fourth to thank you for your letter . . . and for the assistance you rendered [a British naval vessel]. The King . . . further commands me to thank you for your present, and in return, he desires you will accept a suit of armour, such as was worn in former times by his warriors.'

The chiefs Hongi Hika and Waikato with the missionary Thomas Kendall in England, 1820. Kendall began to put the Maori language into written form. Up to 1840 the missionaries printed almost all the reading material available in Maori – the Bible and the Anglican catechism.

Marsden's opinion of Maori

Marsden believed that trade would lead to Maori dependence on Europeans and open the way to Christianity. He planned the first mission station, which was set up at the Bay of Islands in 1814. He had a high opinion of the Maori:

> The natives of New Zealand are far advanced in Civilization, and apparently prepared for receiving the Knowledge of Christianity more than any Savage nations I have seen. Their Habits of Industry are very strong; and their thirst for Knowledge great, they only want the means.
>
> The more I see of these people, the more I am pleased with, and astonished at their moral Ideas, and Characters. They appear like a superior Race of men.

They often met the governor and expected this personal relationship with the Crown's representative to continue. Some wanted to visit the King himself and a few did. Hongi and Waikato met King George IV in 1820.

Between 1814 and 1839 Marsden visited New Zealand seven times. He and the missionaries encouraged Maori to believe that the British monarch had a special interest in protecting them from other foreign nations. In 1831 thirteen northern chiefs, afraid of a possible French invasion, petitioned King William IV for protection. But Europeans were also looking for protection in New Zealand. Sydney traders complained that their business was often risky because of fighting among rival groups they were trading with. They wanted more favourable conditions of trade. But no chief had authority over the whole country, or even large parts of it, and there was no central government to whom traders could appeal, as in England.

Violent events

In 1830 Marsden and Governor Ralph Darling became anxious about a growing trade in preserved heads, which Maori were selling to Europeans. They were afraid that this trade was setting at risk a good Maori–European trade relationship.

The same year one particular incident made the problem of controlling Europeans in New Zealand an urgent one. The English captain and crew of the *Elizabeth* entered into a trade deal with Ngati Toa chief, Te Rauparaha. In return for a cargo of flax, they took him and his war party to the South Island to wreak vengeance on unsuspecting Ngai Tahu living at Akaroa. Many were killed including Tamaiharanui, a most important chief, who was tortured to death.

Two Maori travelled to Sydney to lodge a protest with the governor about the behaviour of the English captain and crew, but the culprits were not punished. While officials and lawyers argued over whether British law covered British subjects in New Zealand, the *Elizabeth*'s captain jumped bail. Marsden told Governor Darling that the Maori people were looking for British protection from this kind of 'outrage', in which Europeans took sides in tribal fighting. Merchants, missionaries, and others complained too. Darling in turn recommended to the Colonial Office in London that a British Resident be appointed in New Zealand. The Colonial Office agreed and appointed James Busby to the position.

A British Resident and a national flag

James Busby arrived in May 1833 at the Bay of Islands, where there was a small settlement of Europeans. He settled at Waitangi. His main duties were to protect 'well-disposed' traders and settlers, to check 'outrages' on the Maori, and to apprehend escaped convicts. But he had no means of enforcing his authority. Europeans in the Bay of Islands in

Te Rauparaha in 1842. With his people he had migrated from Kawhia to the Kapiti coast in the 1820s, one of a number of large migrations of Maori from Waikato and Taranaki districts. By 1840 Pakeha regarded Te Rauparaha as the most powerful chief in the Kapiti region.

James Busby in 1831. He wrote many letters from New Zealand, usually expressing his powerlessness to do anything. In 1835, Busby told his superiors in New South Wales that: 'As far as has been ascertained every acre of land in this country is appropriated among the different tribes; and every individual in the tribe has a distinct interest in the property; although his possession may not always be separately defined.'

1837 set up a vigilante association to protect themselves, very often from each other.

Busby, however, did try to introduce what his instructions called 'a settled form of government' among the Maori. He started by holding a great gathering at Waitangi in March 1834. Chiefs were invited to choose a national flag, so that ships built in New Zealand could be recognised, according to the law of the sea. Three flags were displayed on short poles and voted on, the winning one hoisted, and a twenty-one gun salute fired. From then on Busby arranged for New Zealand-built ships to be registered in the name of the independent tribes of New Zealand; the ships flew the flag. It was also flown on shore, especially at the Bay of Islands. Maori saw it as official acknowledgement of their separate identity.

The Declaration of Independence

Busby called a second meeting when he heard that a Frenchman, Baron de Thierry, was planning to set up his own independent state at Hokianga. On 28 October 1835 he persuaded thirty-four northern chiefs to sign a Declaration of the Independence of New Zealand. They called themselves the Confederation of United Tribes. They asked the British government to recognise the country's independence and to extend Crown protection. The British government agreed to both. Chiefs from further south were invited to join the confederation and an annual congress at Waitangi was proposed. However, even though Busby went on collecting signatures, the congress never met. Continuing competition and war between the tribes prevented that.

William Hobson

In 1837 Governor Richard Bourke sent a naval captain, William Hobson, to investigate fighting among Bay of Islands Maori; it was possibly a threat to trade and people's lives. Bourke asked Hobson, and Busby too, to write reports on New Zealand. Hobson suggested that, to make traders and other British subjects more secure, Britain might take over several sites for settlement; but an arrangement for that would have to be negotiated with the Maori leaders of those areas. He talked of a treaty. Busby suggested a 'protectorate' over the whole country. This would mean that chiefs would continue to lead their people and deal with Europeans, but they would be guided by British officials, who in many ways would be the real rulers of the country (or so Busby thought).

11

The two reports, with letters and petitions from traders to back them up, all arrived at London's Colonial Office in December 1837. They painted a sad, though somewhat exaggerated, picture of a country troubled by Maori fighting, by British subjects committing crimes, and by disagreements between Maori and Pakeha - such as over theft, trade deals, and the straying of livestock into Maori cultivations. With no force to back him, Busby could not solve these problems.

The New Zealand national flag, 1834, flying at the Bay of Islands. The flag was white, with a red Saint George's cross and, in the upper corner on the left side, a blue field with a red cross and four white stars. The present flag of the Maori Women's Welfare League is very similar.

William Hobson. After his 1837 visit to New Zealand he had written to his wife, Liz, that he thought British intervention was needed to keep other nations out, to protect settlers, and to restrain their violence. He also mentioned that the Maori people seemed to be declining rapidly in numbers through European diseases (which was true), and that there was a great deal of British labour and capital invested in the country. He was in favour of Britain's move to set up a colony.

The Colonial Office was at number 14 Downing Street, close to the present British prime minister's residence. It handled most of the official business of British colonies. The building was demolished in 1876.

Plans for settlement

At the same time, London officials were looking at the plans of a private group, called the New Zealand Company, for sending British settlers to New Zealand. The company was meant to get the government's permission to go ahead with such plans, but it went ahead anyway. In May 1839 the company's ship *Tory* left England with a party of people on board who were to buy land for settlement at Port Nicholson (Wellington). The first of several shiploads of emigrants left in September.

The British government had already decided to take action. Officials feared that Maori would resist settlement on any big scale. They were also afraid that violence might erupt when settlers and Maori tried to live close to each other. The British record of dealings with native peoples in other colonies had just been made public; it was not good, and the government wanted to do better in New Zealand.

Questions of sovereignty

The government decided to set up a British colony; but, since Britain had recognised the country as independent, the government felt it could not just take power over New Zealand. The chiefs would resent and fight this too. So they would have to be persuaded to transfer their 'sovereignty' to the British Crown. This was to be the task of Captain Hobson, the newly appointed consul to New Zealand.

Hobson leaves for New Zealand

In August 1839 Hobson sailed for New Zealand. He was given authority to make a treaty agreement with Maori leaders for sovereignty over all or part of the country. His instructions from Lord Normanby, the Secretary of State for the Colonies, told him to get the 'free and intelligent consent' of chiefs to the treaty and to deal with them 'openly'. These instructions also explained, apologetically, why Britain had decided to make a colony in New Zealand – not only because of the 2000 settlers already there, but to control the thousands of expected emigrants and to protect the rights of the Maori people too.

This explanation revealed the change in attitudes of the government. When officials had first thought about plans for a British colony in New Zealand, it was for a Maori New Zealand in which settlers would somehow be accommodated. But by the time Hobson got his instructions, the plan was for a settler New Zealand in which the Maori people would have a special 'protected' position.

In Sydney Hobson was sworn in by Governor George Gipps as lieutenant governor of any territory he might acquire in New Zealand. Hobson chose a small group of officials to go with him and sailed for New Zealand on 18 January 1840.

> No te 30 o nga ra o Hanuere, 1840.
>
> E taku hoa aroha,
>
> Tenei ano taku ki a koe; na, tenei ano tetahi kaipuke manawa kua u mai nei, me tetahi Rangatira ano kei runga, no te Kuini o Ingarani ia, hei Kawana hoki mo tatou. Na, e mea ana ia, kia huihuia katoatia mai nga Rangatira o te Wakaminenga o Nu Tireni, a te Wenerei i tenei wiki tapu e haere ake nei, kia kitekite ratou i a ia. Koia ahau ka mea atu nei ki a koe, e hoa, kia haere mai koe ki konei ki Waitangi, ki taku kainga ano, ki tenei huihuinga. He Rangatira hoki koe no taua Wakaminenga tahi. Heoi ano, ka mutu taku,
>
> Naku,
>
> Na tou hoa aroha,
>
> Na te PUHIPI.

This is the invitation sent by James Busby to Tamati Waka Nene, inviting him to Waitangi. In Busby's name, the invitation asked the recipient, as a chief of the confederation (whakaminenga) to attend a meeting (huihuinga) with the 'chief of the Queen' who had arrived to be a governor for everyone.

Making a Treaty

Preparing the treaty

The *Herald* dropped anchor off Kororareka on Wednesday, 29 January. Busby hurried on board to welcome Hobson and offered to organise a meeting of chiefs at his Waitangi home the following Wednesday.

Over the next four to five days, Hobson had to decide on the wording of the treaty he had been ordered to make with the chiefs. He felt very awkward about this task. He had no legal training.

With the help of his secretary he wrote out some notes. Several missionaries gave their advice. When Busby saw the notes he felt that they were not adequate for a treaty and offered to provide a new draft. Hobson received it on 3 February.

Busby had added an important promise: that Britain would guarantee Maori possession of their lands, their forests, their fisheries and other prized possessions. Without that promise he was sure no one would sign.

The first and second parts of the treaty covered the things that Britain wanted: that the chiefs would give up 'sovereignty', that is, the right to exercise power and authority over everyone in the country; and that Britain would take complete control over all business dealings in land, both buying it from the Maori people, and selling it to settlers.

The third part offered the Maori 'all the rights and privileges of British subjects' – something that English people thought would mean a great deal to anyone.

Hobson asked Henry Williams to translate the treaty into Maori, which he did, with the help of his 21-year-old son Edward, on the evening of 4 February.

Waitangi – Wednesday, 5 February

Most of what we know about what happened next comes from the letters and diaries of some of the missionaries and other people who were at the meeting, including Busby and Hobson.

From early morning that day Maori groups had been arriving at Waitangi. The bay was alive with canoes, converging from all directions, each with thirty or more rowers keeping time to the stroke. Settlers' boats were joining the stream and ships had all their flags flying. Summer showers had cleared and the day was brilliantly fine; cicadas shrilled noisily.

Outside Busby's grounds, stalls were being set up to sell refreshments – pork, cold roasts, pies, baskets of bread, and stout, ale, brandy, and rum.

Special provisions were ready for Maori guests – a half-ton of flour, five tons of potatoes, thirty pigs, and other goods.

On the Waitangi lawn the officers of the *Herald* had erected an enormous marquee. About forty to fifty metres in length, it was made of ships' sails and was decorated with flags. Three or four Sydney mounted police, who had arrived on the *Herald*, paraded in their scarlet uniforms. Hundreds of Maori were sitting in their tribal groups, smoking and talking. Some had come from long distances and carried guns. Little parties of Europeans were strolling up and down – the *Herald*'s officers, missionaries, traders, sailors. The crowd buzzed with excitement.

At about nine o'clock Hobson stepped ashore on the Waitangi beach. With the captain of the *Herald*, Joseph Nias, he walked up the hill to Busby's home. He then went into a room with Busby and Henry Williams to look over the translated treaty. However, as Hobson did not know any Maori, he could not tell if the translation was accurate.

Henry Williams, known to the Maori as Te Wiremu and as 'Karu wha' – 'Four-eyes' – because of his spectacles. The explanations of the treaty given by Williams were most important to Maori understanding, or lack of it. Although many Maori could read and write in Maori by 1840, few would have had a chance to read the treaty before signing it.

The first meeting

Late in the morning the official party moved in procession from Busby's house to the marquee. On a raised platform at one end Hobson sat down at a table covered with the Union Jack. Others took up positions wherever they could. The tent filled rapidly. Over 200 Maori took up the main space. William Colenso, the printer at the nearby Paihia mission station, looked over the scene and wrote:

> In front of the platform, in the foreground, were the principal
> . . . chiefs of several tribes, some clothed with [black and white
> striped] dogskin mats . . . others . . . in . . . new woollen cloaks

A reconstruction of the seating at the Waitangi meeting on 5 February, as described by some who were there.

Positions in the marquee at Waitangi meeting of 5 February

1. William Hobson
2. Joseph Nias
3. James Busby
4. Henry Williams
5. Richard Taylor
6. Jean-Baptiste-Francois Pompallier
7. Priest
8. Wesleyans
9. Willoughby Shortland
10. Church missionaries
11. Officers
12. Hobson's suite
13. Maori
14. Europeans

. . . of crimson, blue, brown, and plaid, and, indeed, of every shade of striking colour . . . while some were dressed in plain European and some in common Native dresses . . . here and there a . . . taiaha, a chief's staff of rank, was seen erected, adorned with the long flowing white hair of the tails of the New Zealand dog and crimson cloth and red feathers.

Felton Mathew commented on the women among the chiefs: 'Their ears were decorated with white feathers or the entire wing of a bird.'

A hush fell as Hobson began. He first spoke to the Europeans, telling them briefly what he was about to do. Then he turned to the Maori people to talk about the treaty. He spoke in English with Williams translating into Maori. He explained that the British people were free to go wherever they chose, and the Queen was always ready to protect them. She was also ready to restrain them, but her efforts were futile because outside British territory she had no authority to do so.

17

'Her Majesty the Queen asks you to sign this treaty,' he said, 'and so give her that power which shall enable her to restrain them.'

He went on, 'I'll give you time to consider the proposal I'll now offer you. What I want you to do is expressly for your own good as you will soon see by the treaty. You yourselves have often asked the King to extend his protection [to you]. Her Majesty now offers that protection in this treaty.'

He finished by reading the treaty in English. Then Williams read the Maori treaty. He said later that he told the chiefs to listen carefully and he explained each part to them. He warned them not to be in a hurry.

'This is Queen Victoria's act of love to you,' he said. 'She wants to ensure that you keep what is yours – your property, your rights and privileges, and those things you value. Who knows when a foreign power, perhaps the French, might try to take this country? The treaty is really like a fortress to you.'

Debate

For over five hours through the heat of the day, chiefs spoke for and against the proposal. Their main concerns were about their authority, their land, and trade dealings.

Rewa said, 'The Maori people don't want a governor! We aren't European. It's true that we've sold some of our lands. But this country is still ours! We chiefs govern this land of our ancestors.'

Kawiti and others echoed these comments.

'Governor,' said Hakiro, striding up and down, 'some might tell you to stay here, but I say this is not the place for you. We are not your people. We are free. We don't need you and we don't want you.'

Tareha joined in: 'We chiefs are the rulers and we won't be ruled over. If we were all to have a rank equal to you that might be acceptable. But if we are going to be subordinate to you, then I say get back to your ship and sail away.'

Many objected strongly to the land purchases that Europeans, especially the missionaries, had made. Hobson promised that all lands unjustly purchased would be returned to the Maori owners.

'That's good,' said Moka. 'That's as it should be. But we'll see what happens. Who will really listen to you? Who's going to obey you? The lands won't be returned.'

Williams, uneasy about this attack on the missionaries, explained to the Europeans present that all land sales before

Tamati Waka Nene had been closely associated with the Methodist missionaries in the Hokianga in the 1830s. A year or so before the treaty signing he had become a Christian. This portrait is by Gottfried Lindauer.

1840 were going to be investigated. Hobson had actually announced this at a large meeting of Europeans, held at Kororareka on 30 January.

Whai complained about Pakeha traders.

'What will you do about trade dealings, and the cheating, lying, and stealing of the whites?' he said.

He also touched on another matter that deeply angered the Maori people: 'Yesterday I was cursed by a white man. Is that the way things are going to be?'

Hobson felt that the feeling of the meeting was running against him. Only a very few chiefs had welcomed him. Rawiri Taiwhanga was one.

'It's a good thing that you have come to be a governor for us,' he said. 'If you stay we will have peace.'

Hone Heke was another.

'Governor,' he said, 'you should stay with us and be like a father. If you go away, then the French or the rum sellers will take us Maori over. How can we know what the future will bring? If you stay, we can be "all as one" with you and the missionaries.'

But now the Hokianga chief, Tamati Waka Nene, rose and turned towards the chiefs.

'I'm going to speak first to you,' he said. 'Some of you tell Hobson to go. But that's not going to solve our difficulties. We have already sold so much of our land here in the north. We have no way of controlling the Europeans who have settled on it. I'm amazed to hear you telling him to go! Why didn't you tell the traders and grog-sellers to go years ago? There are too many Europeans here now, and there are children that unite both our races.'

He looked at Hobson. 'Don't be too concerned with what these others are saying. We need you as a friend, a judge, a peacemaker, and as governor. You must preserve our customs, and never permit our lands to be taken from us.'

Patuone, his brother, agreed.

But Te Kemara leapt up and cried out, 'No! Go back to your own land. It would be all right if we were going to be equal in rank and power, but if you are going to be above us, I say no. Will we end up like this?' And he crossed his hands as if handcuffed. Then suddenly he seized Hobson's hand, shaking it over and over, and roaring out in English, 'How d'ye do, eh, Governor? How d'ye do, eh, Mister Governor?'

Everyone – Maori and Pakeha – was convulsed with laughter, and Hobson decided that it was a good time to adjourn the meeting. They would meet again on the Friday.

Discussion into the night

That evening Maori groups camped on the flat land near the Waitangi river mouth. Talk centred on the treaty. As Williams remembered:

> There was considerable excitement amongst the people, greatly increased by . . . ill-disposed Europeans, stating to the chiefs . . . that their country was gone, and they now were only taurekareka (slaves). Many came to us to speak upon this new state of affairs. We gave them but one version, explaining clause by clause, showing the advantage to them of being taken under the fostering care of the British Government, by which act they would become one people with the English, in the suppression of wars, and of every lawless act; under one Sovereign, and one Law, human and divine.

No one knows what else was said in the discussions that night, but by Thursday morning most chiefs were keen to get the treaty signed immediately so they could go home.

William Colenso. He was looking for a chance to speak on the morning of the signing at Waitangi. He knew that many chiefs had arrived late on 5 February or early on 6 February. They had missed the many discussions and explanations. He was worried that the Maori were placing too much trust on missionary advice to sign. If they did not fully understand the treaty, then their agreement would not be 'their free and intelligent consent'.

Hone Heke and Patuone. After the signing on 6 February, Patuone presented Hobson with a greenstone mere for Queen Victoria. The two men were friends from Hobson's previous visit. They dined together on the *Herald* where, we are told, the officers danced a quadrille, to the tune of two fiddlers, until dark.

Some had already gone. Food was running short. Some of the missionaries, afraid that the chiefs would leave without signing, probably suggested another meeting with Hobson that day. William Colenso suspected that someone had recalled the saying 'Strike while the iron's hot'.

The signing – Thursday, 6 February
The change of plan caught Hobson by surprise. He was summoned ashore late in the morning, arriving in plain clothes, having hastily snatched up his plumed hat. Several

21

hundred Maori were waiting for him in the marquee and more stood around outside. Only Busby and a few Europeans had turned up, among them the Catholic Bishop Pompallier.

Hobson was nervous and uneasy. Feeling that he was being rushed into this unplanned meeting, he rose and said, 'I will only accept signatures today. I can't allow discussion because this meeting hasn't been publicly announced.'

On the table lay a tidily written copy of the treaty in Maori. Williams read it out once more, but, before anyone could sign, Bishop Pompallier asked Hobson for a public assurance that people in New Zealand could follow whatever religion they chose. Hobson agreed and asked Williams to give it, which he did; he included Maori custom.

Then, just as Heke was about to sign, William Colenso asked, 'Your Excellency, do you think the chiefs really understand all aspects of the treaty?'

'If they don't,' said Hobson, 'it's not my fault. I've done all I can. Williams has read it to them in Maori.'

Colenso agreed but pointed out that it had not been explained adequately and he was afraid of a Maori reaction.

'Mr Colenso,' Hobson replied, 'I am sure you will work to avoid that. We've done the best we can.'

The signing went ahead. Busby called each chief by name from a list he had. It was probably Williams who told Hobson to try a few words in Maori. When each chief had signed, Hobson shook hands with him and said, 'He iwi tahi tatou.'

Williams must have known that the words – 'we are one people' – would have a special meaning for the chiefs, especially those who were Christian: Maori and British would be linked, as subjects of the Queen and as followers of Christ.

Over forty Maori leaders signed the treaty parchment with their names or their moko that afternoon. As the signing was drawing to a close, a chief gave a signal for three thundering cheers which closed the meeting.

Colenso was left to distribute gifts – two blankets and some tobacco to each person signing.

Reports and celebrations
Hobson, pleased about the outcome of the meeting, immediately wrote a letter on it to his superiors in London. 'I assured them in the most fervent manner that they might rely implicitly on the good faith of Her Majesty's government,' he wrote. He told his superiors that he had got the agreement of twenty-six of the chiefs who had signed the Declaration of Independence in 1835.

Locations of treaty signings

National Archives (Wellington) holds the treaty sheets which are listed below. In 1877 they were first published in *Facsimiles . . . of the Treaty of Waitangi*. The sheets are numbered according to the sequence in which they are found in the *Facsimiles*. The names attributed to the sheets here are not part of any official record. The list indicates the place of signing, the dates or date of signing, and gives approximate numbers of signatures.

There is a further printed sheet which has several signatures and is witnessed by R. Maunsell. It may date from an 1844 printing of the treaty however.

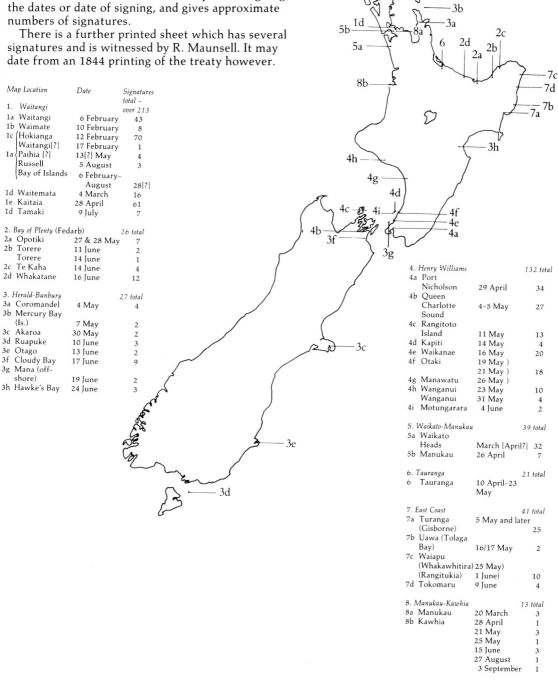

Map Location	Date	Signatures
		total – over 213
1. Waitangi		
1a Waitangi	6 February	43
1b Waimate	10 February	8
1c Hokianga	12 February	70
Waitangi[?]	17 February	1
1a Paihia [?]	13[?] May	4
Russell	5 August	3
Bay of Islands	6 February–August	28[?]
1d Waitemata	4 March	16
1e Kaitaia	28 April	61
1d Tamaki	9 July	7
2. Bay of Plenty (Fedarb)		26 total
2a Opotiki	27 & 28 May	7
2b Torere	11 June	2
Torere	14 June	1
2c Te Kaha	14 June	4
2d Whakatane	16 June	12
3. Herald-Bunbury		27 total
3a Coromandel	4 May	4
3b Mercury Bay (Is.)	7 May	2
3c Akaroa	30 May	2
3d Ruapuke	10 June	3
3e Otago	13 June	2
3f Cloudy Bay	17 June	9
3g Mana (off-shore)	19 June	2
3h Hawke's Bay	24 June	3

Map Location	Date	Signatures
4. Henry Williams		132 total
4a Port Nicholson	29 April	34
4b Queen Charlotte Sound	4–5 May	27
4c Rangitoto Island	11 May	13
4d Kapiti	14 May	4
4e Waikanae	16 May	20
4f Otaki	19 May) 21 May)	18
4g Manawatu	26 May)	
4h Wanganui	23 May	10
Wanganui	31 May	4
4i Motungarara	4 June	2
5. Waikato-Manukau		39 total
5a Waikato Heads	March [April?]	32
5b Manukau	26 April	7
6. Tauranga		21 total
6 Tauranga	10 April–23 May	
7. East Coast		41 total
7a Turanga (Gisborne)	5 May and later	25
7b Uawa (Tolaga Bay)	16/17 May	2
7c Waiapu (Whakawhitira)	25 May)	
(Rangitukia)	1 June)	10
7d Tokomaru	9 June	4
8. Manukau-Kawhia		13 total
8a Manukau	20 March	3
8b Kawhia	28 April	1
	21 May	3
	25 May	1
	15 June	3
	27 August	1
	3 September	1

That, he wrote, 'must be deemed a full and clear recognition of the sovereign rights of Her Majesty over the northern parts of this island.'

He was lucky. The following day there was torrential rain and no one could leave the ship. On Saturday 8 February the *Herald* ran up all her flags and fired a twenty-one gun salute in honour of the new British colony of New Zealand.

Hobson was anticipating full Maori agreement to the treaty elsewhere.

The signing at Mangungu

Hobson set out to obtain more signatures. He went first to Waimate and then on to the Hokianga. Leaders from both places had been at Waitangi and some had signed there.

At Mangungu on the Hokianga Harbour, hundreds of Maori gathered, among them chiefs who were used to negotiating business contracts with Europeans.

'We are glad to see the governor,' said Te Taonui, 'but let him be a governor for the Pakeha. We'll be our own governor. How do the Pakeha behave to the blacks of Port Jackson? They treat them like dogs: a Pakeha kills a pig – the black comes to the door and eats the refuse.'

Te Taonui knew. He had visited Sydney. Chiefs at Waitangi, too, had mentioned British treatment of Aborigines.

Chiefs told Hobson they were suspicious of British motives for making a treaty.

'We think you are going to deceive us,' said Mohi. 'The Pakeha tell us so. Where do you get your authority from anyway? Is it from the Queen? If you do come as governor, you had better stop all our lands falling into Pakeha hands.

A view of the feast given by Hobson on 13 February, the day after the treaty signing at Hokianga. The feast was held at Horeke, a well-established timbermilling site, about two kilometres from Mangungu. The all-day feast began with a haka of 1500 men, which the official party were asked to view from boats anchored offshore. About 3000 enjoyed pork, potatoes, rice, and sugar. Blankets and tobacco were given to chiefs. The Horeke guns fired a small salute, answered by a volley from a local trader.

I want everyone to hear that. It's only right to say what we think.'

'We are not willing to give up our land,' Te Taonui said. 'The land is like a parent to us. We obtain all things from it. The land is our chieftainship. We will not give it up.'

Other chiefs spoke about trade, both its benefits and its problems.

After eight hours of debate, chiefs started to sign. John Hobbs, a local missionary who was interpreter, believed that the promises given by Hobson were decisive. He had translated Hobson's 'repeated assurances . . . that the Queen did not want the land, but merely the sovereignty, that . . . her officers might be more able more effectively to govern her subjects . . . and punish those of them who might be guilty of crime.'

He also pledged that the land would 'never be forcibly taken' and gave Hobson's 'most solemn assurance' that the Queen's government would always act with 'truth and justice'.

These explanations shaped Maori understanding, one chief referring to the treaty as a 'very sacred' deed which he must take care of.

Hobson looks for more signatures

Over the next months more important chiefs in the Bay of Islands signed the treaty. In the meantime Hobson sailed south in his search for signatures. He stopped first at the Waitemata Harbour, but suddenly he was taken ill. Henry Williams, who was with the group, helped organise a signing, and the *Herald* sailed back with the sick Hobson to the Bay of Islands.

One of Hobson's officials now took over the job of getting signatures. Several copies of the treaty in Maori were written out. Some were sent to missionaries who were asked to call treaty meetings. Others were taken on long journeys by people such as Henry Williams, the army men, Thomas Bunbury and W.C. Symonds, and a trader, James Fedarb.

The signing of the treaty at the entrance to the Tamaki river, probably at Karaka Bay. Waitemata–Hauraki Gulf chiefs signed on 4 March and 9 July, both times possibly there.

KO WIKITORIA, te Kuini o Ingarani, i tana mahara atawai ki nga Rangatira me nga Hapu o Nu-Tirani, i tana hiahia hoki kia tohungia ki a ratou o ratou rangatiratanga, me to ratou wenua, a kia mau tonu hoki te Rongo ki a ratou me te ata noho hoki, kua wakaaro ia he mea tika kia tukua mai tetahi Rangatira hei kai wakarite ki nga Tangata Maori o Nu-Tirani. Kia wakaaetia e nga Rangatira Maori te Kawanatanga o te Kuini, ki nga wahi katoa o te wenua nei, me nga motu. Na te mea hoki he tokomaha ke nga tangata o tona iwi kua noho ki tenei wenua, a e haere mai nei.

Na, ko te Kuini e hiahia ana kia wakaritea te Kawanatanga, kia kaua ai nga kino e puta mai ki te Tangata Maori ki te Pakeha e noho ture kore ana.

Na, kua pai te Kuini kia tukua ahau, a WIREMU HOPIHONA, he Kapitana i te Roiara Nawi, hei Kawana mo nga wahi katoa o Nu-Tirani, e tukua aianei a mua atu ki te Kuini; e mea atu ana ia ki nga Rangatira o te Wakaminenga o nga Hapu o Nu-Tirani, me era Rangatira atu, enei Ture ka korerotia nei :—

Ko te Tuatahi,

Ko nga Rangatira o te Wakaminenga, me nga Rangatira katoa hoki, kihai i uru ki taua Wakaminenga, ka tuku rawa atu ki te Kuini o Ingarani ake tonu atu te Kawanatanga katoa o o ratou wenua.

Ko te Tuarua,

Ko te Kuini o Ingarani ka wakarite ka wakaae ki nga Rangatira, ki nga Hapu, ki nga Tangata katoa o Nu-Tirani, te tino Rangatiratanga o o ratou wenua, o ratou kainga, me o ratou taonga katoa. Otiia ko nga Rangatira o te Wakaminenga, me nga Rangatira katoa atu, ka tuku ki te Kuini te hokonga o era wahi wenua e pai ai te tangata nona te wenua, ki te ritenga o te utu e wakaritea ai e ratou ko te kai hoko e meatia nei e te Kuini hei kai hoko mona.

Ko te Tuatoru,

Hei wakaritenga mai hoki tenei mo te wakaaetanga ki te Kawanatanga o te Kuini. Ka tiakina e te Kuini o Ingarani nga Tangata Maori katoa o Nu-Tirani. Ka tukua ki a ratou nga tikanga katoa rite tahi ki ana mea ki nga tangata o Ingarani.

(SIGNED)

WILLIAM HOBSON, Consul & Lieutenant-Governor.

Na, ko matou, ko nga Rangatira o te Wakaminenga o nga Hapu o Nu-Tirani, ka huihui nei ki Waitangi. Ko matou hoki ko nga Rangatira o Nu-Tirani, ka kite nei i te ritenga o enei kupu, ka tangohia, ka wakaaetia katoatia e matou. Koia ka tohungia ai o matou ingoa o matou tohu.

Ka meatia tenei ki Waitangi, i te ono o nga ra o Pepuere, i te Tau kotahi mano, ewaru rau, ewa tekau o to tatou Ariki.

KA TAIA I TE PEREHI I PAIHIA.

Hobson had 200 copies of the treaty in Maori printed on 17 February. The same day Pomare signed the treaty and over the next months Hobson kept collecting signatures in the Bay of Islands – among them the great chiefs Kawiti and Iwikau of Ngati Tuwharetoa in the centre of the North Island.

Some of the negotiators were not experienced in New Zealand ways. Major Bunbury, for example, became impatient at lengthy discussions. But the missionaries who took part often knew the tribes well and understood many of their customs. For instance, they knew that women could be highly influential in Maori affairs. Henry Williams had two women sign his treaty copy, but he told Hobson that other women

A copy of the treaty taken to the East Coast of the North Island.

HMS *Herald* in Sylvan Cove, Stewart Island, June 1840. The drawing was made by Edward Marsh Williams, who had helped to translate the treaty at Paihia, and who accompanied Major Bunbury as his interpreter.

The missionaries involved in treaty negotiations allowed several women to sign. This portrait by Gottfried Lindauer is of Rangi Topeora who signed at Kapiti. Kahe Te Rau-o-te-rangi signed at Wellington, and Rere-o-maki at Wanganui. Ana Hamu signed the Waitangi sheet and Ereonora signed at Kaitaia.

complained that they were not allowed to play a more prominent part.

'After all,' one said indignantly, 'the other partner to the treaty is a woman – Queen Victoria!'

One woman of rank who signed was Ereonora, the wife of Nopera Panakareao. Nopera had prepared carefully for the meeting at Kaitaia at the end of April. He questioned missionaries and officials about the wording of the treaty, especially about the word used for 'sovereignty' – kawanatanga.

At the meeting he explained it to his people in this way: 'Only the shadow of the land passes to the Queen. The substance stays with us, the Maori people.'

Bill of 1 July 1840			
28 May	Opotiki	8lbs tobacco @ 3/-	1.4.0
		12 pipes @ ½d	6
15 June	Te Kaha	5 fancy pipes @ 2/6	12.6
		½lb tobacco	1.6
16 June	Torere	2 fancy pipes @ 2/6	5.0
		½lb tobacco	1.6
17 June	Whakatane	11 fancy pipes	1.17.6
		4 ditto boxes	8.0
		3 looking glasses	4.6
		5lbs tobacco	15.0
		4 rows beads	2.0
		1 slate	2.0
			£5.4.0

James Fedarb was a trader in the Bay of Plenty. He was asked by Tauranga missionaries to get chiefs' agreement in that region. This is the bill he lodged for gifts given.

The full moko of Tuhawaiki. Bunbury reported: 'Tuhawaiki came on board in the full dress staff uniform of a British aide-de-camp, with gold lace trousers, cocked hat and plume, . . . accompanied by [his] orderly sergeant.' The chief spoke English and wanted to sign the treaty immediately. He wanted the British government to confirm his tribe's ownership of their land and he also wanted to register his 25-ton vessel.

'We now have a man at the helm,' he said. 'Before, everyone wanted to steer. First one said, "Let me steer!" and then another, "Let me steer!" But we never went straight. Now we have a steersman.'

Proclaiming British sovereignty

Meanwhile, a large group of settlers from England who had arrived at Port Nicholson started to set up their own government, even though they knew about Hobson's negotiations. Hobson saw their actions as disloyal to the Queen, and a challenge to him and his work. According to international law, he was the only one who had the authority to set up a British colony in New Zealand. So, on 21 May, he proclaimed British sovereignty over the whole of the country: over the North Island, because he considered that

Te Tiriti o Waitangi

Ko Wikitoria te Kuini o Ingarani i tana mahara atawai ki nga Rangatira me nga Hapu o Nu Tirani i tana hiahia hoki kia tohungia ki a ratou o ratou rangatiratanga me to ratou wenua, a kia mau tonu hoki te Rongo ki a ratou me te Atanoho hoki kua wakaaro ia he mea tika kia tukua mai tetahi Rangatira – hei kai wakarite ki nga Tangata maori o Nu Tirani – kia wakaaetia e nga Rangatira maori te Kawanatanga o te Kuini ki nga wahikatoa o te wenua nei me nga motu – na te mea hoki he tokomaha ke nga tangata o tona Iwi Kua noho ki tenei wenua, a e haere mai nei.

Na ko te Kuini e hiahia ana kia wakaritea te Kawanatanga kia kaua ai nga kino e puta mai ki te tangata maori ki te Pakeha e noho ture kore ana.

Na kua pai te Kuini kia tukua a hau a Wiremu Hopihona he Kapitana i te Roiara Nawi hei Kawana mo nga wahi katoa o Nu Tirani e tukua aianei amua atu ki te Kuini, e mea atu ana ia ki nga Rangatira o te wakaminenga o nga hapu o Nu Tirani me era Rangatira atu enei ture ka korerotia nei.

Ko te tuatahi

Ko nga Rangatira o te wakaminenga me nga Rangatira katoa hoki ki hai i uru ki taua wakaminenga ka tuku rawa atu ki te Kuini o Ingarani ake tonu atu – te Kawanatanga katoa o o ratou wenua.

Ko te tuarua

Ko te Kuini o Ingarani ka wakarite ka wakaae ki nga Rangatira ki nga hapu – ki nga tangata katoa o Nu Tirani te tino rangatiratanga o o ratou wenua o ratou kainga me o ratou taonga katoa. Otiia ko nga Rangatira o te wakaminenga me nga Rangatira katoa atu ka tuku ki te Kuini te hokonga o era wahi wenua e pai ai te tangata nona te wenua – ki te ritenga o te utu e wakaritea ai e ratou ko te kai hoko e meatia nei e te Kuini hei kai hoko mona.

Ko te tuatoru

Hei wakaritenga mai hoki tenei mo te wakaaetanga ki te Kawanatanga o te Kuini – Ka tiakina e te Kuini o Ingarani nga tangata maori katoa o Nu Tirani ka tukua ki a ratou nga tikanga katoa rite tahi ki ana mea ki nga tangata o Ingarani.

[signed] W. Hobson Consul & Lieutenant Governor

Na ko matou ko nga Rangatira o te Wakaminenga o nga hapu o Nu Tirani ka huihui nei ki Waitangi ko matou hoki ko nga Rangatira o Nu Tirani ka kite nei i te ritenga o enei kupu. Ka tangohia ka wakaaetia katoatia e matou, koia ka tohungia ai o matou ingoa o matou tohu.

Ka meatia tenei ki Waitangi i te ono o nga ra o Pepueri i te tau kotahi mano e waru rau e wa te kau o to tatou Ariki.

This treaty text was signed at Waitangi, 6 February 1840, and thereafter in the north and at Auckland. It is reproduced as it was written, except for the heading above the chiefs' names: ko nga Rangatira o te Wakaminenga.

The treaty in Maori and English — some differences

Article 1

By the treaty in English, Maori leaders gave the Queen 'all the rights and power of sovereignty' over their land.

By the treaty in Maori, they gave the Queen 'te kawanatanga katoa' — the complete government over their land.

Article 2

By the treaty in English, Maori leaders and people, collectively and individually, were confirmed in and guaranteed 'exclusive and undisturbed possession of their lands and estates, forests, fisheries, and other properties'.

By the treaty in Maori, they were guaranteed 'te tino rangatiratanga' – the unqualified exercise of their chieftainship over their lands, villages, and all their treasures.

The Treaty of Waitangi

Her Majesty Victoria Queen of the United Kingdom of Great Britain and Ireland regarding with Her Royal Favor the Native Chiefs and Tribes of New Zealand and anxious to protect their just Rights and Property and to secure to them the enjoyment of Peace and Good Order has deemed it necessary in consequence of the great number of Her Majesty's Subjects who have already settled in New Zealand and the rapid extension of Emigration both from Europe and Australia which is still in progress to constitute and appoint a functionary properly authorized to treat with the Aborigines of New Zealand for the recognition of Her Majesty's sovereign authority over the whole or any part of those islands – Her Majesty therefore being desirous to establish a settled form of Civil Government with a view to avert the evil consequences which must result from the absence of the necessary Laws and Institutions alike to the native population and to Her subjects has been graciously pleased to empower and to authorize me William Hobson a Captain in Her Majesty's Royal Navy Consul and Lieutenant Governor of such parts of New Zealand as may be or hereafter shall be ceded to Her Majesty to invite the confederated and independent Chiefs of New Zealand to concur in the following Articles and Conditions.

Article the first

The Chiefs of the Confederation of the United Tribes of New Zealand and the separate and independent Chiefs who have not become members of the Confederation cede to Her Majesty the Queen of England absolutely and without reservation all the rights and powers of Sovereignty which the said Confederation of Individual Chiefs respectively exercise or possess, or may be supposed to exercise or to possess over their respective Territories as the sole sovereigns thereof.

Article the second

Her Majesty the Queen of England confirms and guarantees to the Chiefs and Tribes of New Zealand and to the respective families and individuals thereof the full exclusive and undisturbed possession of their Lands and Estates Forests Fisheries and other properties which they may collectively or individually possess so long as it is their wish and desire to retain the same in their possession; but the Chiefs of the United Tribes and the individual Chiefs yield to Her Majesty the exclusive right of Preemption over such lands as the proprietors thereof may be disposed to alienate at such prices as may be agreed upon between the respective Proprietors and persons appointed by Her Majesty to treat with them in that behalf.

Article the third

In consideration thereof Her Majesty the Queen of England extends to the Natives of New Zealand Her royal protection and imparts to them all the Rights and Privileges of British Subjects.

[signed] W. Hobson Lieutenant Governor

Now therefore We the Chiefs of the Confederation of the United Tribes of New Zealand being assembled in Congress at Victoria in Waitangi and We the Separate and Independent Chiefs of New Zealand claiming authority over the Tribes and Territories which are specified after our respective names, having been made fully to understand the Provisions of the foregoing Treaty, accept and enter into the same in the full spirit and meaning thereof in witness of which we have attached our signatures or marks at the places and the dates respectively specified.

Done at Waitangi this Sixth day of February in the year of Our Lord one thousand eight hundred and forty.

This English text was signed at Waikato Heads in March or April 1840 and at Manukau on 26 April by thirty-nine chiefs only. The text became the 'official' version.

the chiefs who had signed the treaty had ceded it to him; over the South and Stewart Islands on the ground that Cook had 'discovered' them.

Treaty meetings were still going on. On 3 September the last signature was put on a copy of the treaty somewhere near Kawhia. Over 500 chiefs had signed at about fifty meetings.

In October Hobson sent the British government a list of the chiefs who had signed. He also sent them copies of the treaty, in Maori and English. He said nothing about any differences of meaning between them. He probably did not know this himself. But there were important differences.

No unanimous Maori agreement

Hobson also did not draw attention to the fact that a number of very important chiefs had not signed the treaty. Te Wherowhero of Waikato refused to sign, although he was probably asked twice. Symonds, who took the treaty to him, said that Te Wherowhero was offended because he had heard about the celebrations at Waitangi and found the Manukau signing very feeble by comparison. The same was possibly true elsewhere; only in the north was Hobson able to provide the feasting that was fitting on such an important occasion.

The chiefs here are, from left, Mananui and his brother Iwikau of Ngati Tuwharetoa, and Apihai Te Kawau of Ngati Whatua and his nephew, probably Paora Tuhaere. Mananui refused to sign and objected to Iwikau's signing. Apihai Te Kawau signed at Manukau Harbour.

Other chiefs – like Taraia of Thames and Tupaea of Tauranga – refused to sign because they wanted to retain full control over all their affairs. They feared this would be restricted by the governor.

Some chiefs had no chance to say yes or no because the treaty was not offered to them. From Wanganui to Mokau, north of Taranaki, there were no treaty meetings, and most of the chiefs of Hawke's Bay and Wairarapa were not asked to sign.

Te Arawa of Rotorua and Ngati Tuwharetoa of Taupo refused to sign. Mananui Te Heuheu, the great Ngati Tuwharetoa chief, returned the gift of blankets given to his younger brother Iwikau, who had signed at the Bay of Islands. Mananui saw no reason to put his mana under that of a mere woman – the Queen.

At Hokianga one chief brought back to Hobson his gifts of blankets with a letter signed by fifty of his tribe. He wanted his name removed from the treaty. Hobson was highly annoyed and would not listen.

Reasons for signing
Almost everywhere Maori leaders were extremely cautious about giving their agreement to the treaty. Many objected strongly at the treaty meetings but then signed. Others signed willingly.

Why, then, did so many sign?

From what chiefs said, at the time and later, we know that they signed the treaty for one or other of many reasons.

Authority
They expected the treaty to be the start of a new relationship with Britain – one in which they would play an equal role.

They expected officials in New Zealand to control troublesome Europeans.

Chiefs would look after their own people. Their rangatiratanga was safe in the treaty's second clause.

The mana of the land would still be held by the Maori people. It would even be increased by the agreement with the world's major naval power, who might help them against France or other nations.

Most especially they believed that the Queen had a personal authority and that the treaty was a very personal agreement between the Queen herself and the chiefs. Treaty negotiators had explained it that way to get Maori agreement.

Land
The issue of land was usually foremost in influencing chiefs to sign.

Some areas needed support against aggressive European land buyers.

Other areas were quite keen to sell land to the governor.

Many tribes saw a new way of fighting old enemies: if they sold disputed land, they would no longer have to fight their rivals for it.

Many chiefs hoped that the new agreement would bring peace to the country. For instance, Ngati Whatua leaders had travelled to the Bay of Islands shortly after the Waitangi signing to ask Hobson for his protection against their old enemies, Nga Puhi and Waikato. They offered him land on the Waitemata for his government.

Trade and settlement
All who signed hoped for a share in the good things that settlers would bring: more markets for produce, more goods to buy, and a demand for Maori labour and services of all kinds.

They had no idea that the British government planned to bring settlers to the country in large numbers.

The covenant
Above all else, Maori leaders believed that missionary advice was wise and could probably be trusted: the treaty would be good for the country and the people.

They were certainly influenced, too, by the way the treaty was explained to them. The missionaries had been careful to explain the treaty as the personal wish of the Queen – her 'act of love'.

Missionaries, at least at Waitangi, had also presented the treaty as a covenant between the Maori and the Queen, as head of the English church and state. So, many Maori would look on the treaty as a bond similar to the covenants of the Bible. This was very important to them for, by 1840, nearly half the Maori population was following Christian beliefs and ways.

But for Hobson this religious understanding, if he grasped it at all, was just part of the business of getting Maori agreement to a transfer of sovereignty. Britain needed the treaty to reassure the Maori people and to win their co-operation so that British settlement could begin in earnest.

But this was a fish-hook that he kept concealed.

Kawanatanga and Rangatiratanga
Government Authority and Chiefly Authority

Even while the treaty was still being signed in 1840, Maori leaders in the north told Hobson that they were concerned about the future. Hobson tried to calm their fears, but by the end of that year some chiefs were convinced that their freedom was threatened. Government regulations would multiply, they said, and one governor would succeed another until the Maori people were 'ensnared'.

They were right. Hobson had begun to make laws and regulations for 'the peace, order, and good government' of the country. He did this with the advice of six people, all Europeans, who made up a governing council. But as governor he was in sole charge of government, responsible only to the Secretary of State for the Colonies in distant London.

For his dealings with the Maori people, Hobson appointed a Chief Protector of the Maori and several assistant protectors. The protectors' main job was to liaise with Maori communities for the governor. They were supposed to be guardians of Maori welfare, but at the same time had to help the government buy Maori land.

George Clarke, the first protector, soon saw that combining these two things was not helpful to Maori interests. He could also see that government authority and chiefly authority – both agreed to in the treaty – would inevitably clash.

This happened in numerous ways as government regulations and laws began to challenge the right of chiefs to run their own affairs. Late in 1841 Hobson issued a regulation forbidding the felling of kauri. This angered the Hokianga chief Nene who had supported the treaty. A few months later a youth called Maketu was put on trial and hanged for murder

Auckland in 1840 with only a few tents and shelters. A view from roughly the same spot in 1853 shows how quickly the town grew.

– the first real test of whether Maori would accept the British style of justice.

Northern chiefs usually co-operated with the new government. Elsewhere chiefs often rejected government laws and rules as interference. But chiefly authority was also being threatened by the presence and actions of increasing numbers of British settlers.

Settlers

Settlements at Auckland, Wellington, and elsewhere grew more rapidly than any Maori ever imagined. The new settlers were soon pressing the governor to have a say in running their own affairs. But the first governors – Hobson, Robert FitzRoy, and George Grey – knew that the safety of these settlers depended on showing respect for the treaty, and they often repeated its guarantees.

In 1846 the British government proposed a system of government for New Zealand which would give the vote to males who could read and write English. Maori representation was completely left out. At that time, there were only 13 000 settlers living beside a Maori population many times that number. Governor Grey knew that if he set up such a system there would be war. He rejected the proposal.

Nevertheless, in the 1840s the government made more laws and regulations, and continued to expand its activities in such matters as the control of settlements, commerce, and shipping. These were all things that affected Maori communities. Yet there was no place for Maori people in the government. Grey even abolished the Protectorate in 1846. Instead, he established special relationships with certain chiefs, favouring them with gifts and other attentions, and he appointed people to purchase Maori land. By then, numerous difficulties with land had appeared.

Land

From 1840 Maori gradually became aware that they were no longer free to dispose of their lands as they chose. Under the terms of the treaty they could sell land only to the government. If they wanted to sell land and the government did not want to buy it, the land could not be sold to anyone else. If the government agreed to buy the land, officials could force Maori to sell at a low price, and then could sell it to settlers at a much higher price. Maori communities naturally resented these restrictions, and some wrote to the government to appeal against this.

The artist Charles Heaphy painted this view of Wellington in September 1841. The flat section is Te Aro with the Brooklyn hills on the right.

They also found it strange that land could be resold from one settler to another. Before 1840 land had been 'sold' to secure the occupation of a Pakeha who would be useful to the tribe. Land was not a commodity. Now the laws of the new government were forcing Maori to accept that selling land to a Pakeha meant that they had permanently disposed of it and all rights over it. Maori began to raise questions about their rights to fisheries adjacent to land sold, and about such matters as ownership of metals and stones in it, and the resources that grew and lived on it.

The investigation of all pre-1840 land sales caused great agitation among Maori and settler. European and Maori evidence had to be given to justify a settler's claim to a piece of land. Where the sale was fair and the buyer was occupying the land, Maori and settler were usually satisfied.

But some of the large sales, such as those to the New Zealand Company in Wellington, caused serious conflicts between settler and Maori. Wellington Maori fought hard to retain control of papakainga and cultivations in the face of settler efforts to remove the people from the land. Some leaders became incensed as the government tried to push aside Maori claims and allow settlers to take up land. One chief, Wi Tako, wrote numerous letters to officials and newspapers. His evidence helped to prove that the New Zealand Company had not clearly explained to local Maori the terms of the company purchase of Wellington land.

In a number of areas in the early 1840s Maori grew more cautious about land sales. They were not prepared to sell land indiscriminately. They often wanted to retain coastal areas and swamp lands for the resources associated with them.

A PUBLIC MEETING

Will be held at the Exchange, Te Aro, on Wednesday evening, April 20, at 7 o'clock precisely, to consider the late aggressions of the Natives at Porirua, Wanganui, and elsewhere, and the best steps to be taken with regard to the lands chosen by the Colonists and of which they are unable to obtain possession in consequence of the alleged claims of the Natives.

An early attendance is particularly requested.   It is hoped the Company's Principal Agent, the Chief Police Magistrate, and the Protector of Aborigines will attend on this important occasion.

Manners-street, April 16, 1842.

Printed at the " Gazette " Office, Port Nicholson.

This meeting was held because settlers had been incensed at Te Rangihaeata's resistance to surveys of land in his tribal area at Porirua.

Wi Tako Ngatata. One newspaper reported him as saying: 'I ask you Pakeha what did the Queen tell you? Did she say to you "Go to New Zealand and fraudulently take away the land of the natives"? You say no, then why do you encroach upon land that has not been fairly purchased?'

They were reluctant to sell large areas of land, for they wanted to remain close to Pakeha settlement to provide goods and services. They were prepared to tolerate a good deal of settler provocation and make concessions to government; but there was a limit beyond which Maori refused to be pushed in land matters.

This was demonstrated at Wairau in 1843 when settlers, impatient to survey land they considered theirs, would not wait for a proper investigation, which local chiefs expected. In a violent confrontation both settler and Maori lives were lost. In several districts of the North Island there were violent disputes between Maori and settler in the 1840s.

Challenges to British sovereignty

In the far north, beginning in 1844, Hone Heke and his ally Kawiti challenged British authority. More than most Maori leaders they seem to have understood that the shadow of 'sovereignty' over the land was as much a threat to their chieftainship as any outright seizing of the land. In letters to the governor, Heke made one point clearly – he wanted British authority removed. Other northern leaders sided with the government. But the fighting, which brought more troops to the country, proved that the Maori were formidable warriors and capable of inflicting humiliating defeats on British troops.

The Queen and her people

Through the 1840s officials and missionaries soothed Maori fears by arguing that the treaty was a compact between the Queen and the Maori people. During the northern war, Henry

Te Rangihaeata. He was at the forefront of resistance to settler claims to disputed land in Ngati Toa areas in Wellington and Marlborough.

Kawiti. He signed the 1835 Declaration of the Independence of New Zealand. He was reluctant to sign the treaty but was finally persuaded to do so in May 1840.

Williams printed 400 copies of the treaty in Maori and spent many days explaining to Maori groups that, because the treaty was 'a sacred compact', neither the Queen nor the governor would allow any 'tinihanga' (tricky business). At major meetings, Governor Grey repeated the treaty promises and said they would be kept. Maori were very uneasy despite this kind of talk, but they still believed they enjoyed a special relationship with Queen Victoria and with her governors.

Some chiefs wrote to the Queen and sent gifts. Governor Grey, in particular, encouraged Maori to feel that they had a personal relationship with him. The Maori view of government as personal and approachable lasted into the 1850s and 1860s. By that time responsibility for Maori welfare was passing from a 'benevolent' governor to a settler parliament. Holding such a view left Maori leaders ill-equipped to deal with the impersonal kind of government

Ohaeawai. This view of British troops attacking Heke's pa at Ohaeawai was made by Cyprian Bridge, one of the senior officers.

Heke's challenge

In July 1844 the flagstaff at Russell was cut down. Hone Heke was behind this: he saw the signal staff as a tohu (a sign) that New Zealand was passing into British hands. Other northern Maori were also disappointed that the treaty had not brought the expected benefits. When the government had the flagstaff re-erected, it was brought down three more times. Through 1845 and 1846 Heke's challenge to British sovereignty developed into a war between Maori troops, led by Heke and Kawiti, and British troops with Maori allies.

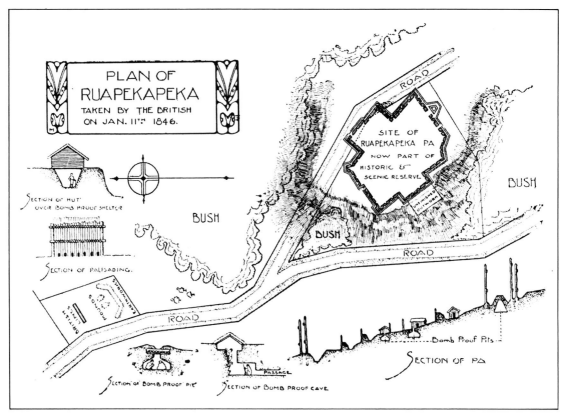

PLAN OF RUAPEKAPEKA TAKEN BY THE BRITISH ON JAN. 11TH 1846.

that began to develop around 1850. But the government and the missionaries were still not fully explaining to Maori the real meaning of Britain's 'rights of sovereignty'.

Pros and cons

By 1850, the balance sheet of benefits and disadvantages brought by the British since 1840 might have appeared favourable to many Maori. They had profited by supplying centres such as Auckland, New Plymouth, and Wellington with produce. They were employed in public works and on private contracts. They built rush cottages for new emigrants.

Ruapekapeka. Kawiti was a superb military strategist. He organised the construction of Ohaeawai and Ruapekapeka pa, developing new structures that would withstand the fiercest attacks by British forces. The British were so impressed by Ruapekapeka that they did this sketch.

A letter to the Queen

The northern war had only just finished when a London official, Earl Grey, ordered that Maori land ownership should be restricted. Four hundred Auckland settlers petitioned for the treaty's land guarantee to be respected as it had been. They were afraid for their safety if the Maori people heard about Grey's idea.

Te Wherowhero also heard about it and wrote to the Queen. Here is his letter and the reply.

Oh Madam,

We salute you, our love is great to you, we have not forgotten your words nor your kind thoughts to all the world. Oh, Madam! listen to our words, all the Chiefs of Waikato. Let your love be towards us, and be kind to us, as Christ also hath loved all. May God incline you to hold fast our words, and we to hold fast yours for ever. Oh Madam, listen! The report has come hither, that your Elders (councillors) think of taking the Maoris land without cause. Behold, the heart is sad, but we will not believe this report, because we heard from the first Governor that with ourselves lay the consideration for our lands, and the second Governor repeated the same, and this Governor also, all their speeches were the same, therefore, we write to you to love our people, write your thoughts to us, that peace may abide with the people of these islands.

From your friend,

Te Wherowhero

From Earl Grey to Governor Grey.

Downing Street,
May 3rd, 1848.

Sir,

You will inform Te Wherowhero and the other chiefs of Te Waikato district who signed the letter to the Queen inclosed in your Despatch of Nov. 13th, 1847, No. 117, that I have laid it before Her Majesty, who has commanded me to express the satisfaction with which she has received this loyal and dutiful address, and to assure them that there is not the slightest foundation for rumours to which they allude and it never was intended that the Treaty of Waitangi should be violated by dispossessing the tribes which are parties to it, of any portion of the land secured to them by the Treaty without their consent. On the contrary Her Majesty has always directed that the Treaty should be most scrupulously and religiously observed. I take this opportunity of referring you to a letter which I have recently addressed to the Wesleyan Missionary Committee in answer to a representation on their part, also enclosed, expressing similar fears of intended infractions of the Treaty of Waitangi. That letter contains a full exposition of my views, both respecting the Treaty itself and also some portions of the general question as to the ownership of land in New Zealand, about which misunderstandings had arisen. I wish to refer you particularly to the explanation which I have there given of the meaning intended to be conveyed by a passage of land instructions.

I have etc,
(signed) GREY.

Money earned by Maori contributed to the welfare of both Maori and settler; shops in centres like Auckland relied on Maori trade. At Otaki, in the Waikato, and elsewhere, rural communities flourished. They had horses and livestock, ploughs, mills, and fields of wheat and other crops.

Maori also took part in the social life of the colony. In Auckland there were regattas, socials at Government House, celebrations for the Queen's birthday and the colony's anniversary day. Churches were established and some provision made for schooling and hospitals.

Not everyone could share in these benefits, however; more remote districts had little to do with these changes. And some Maori leaders were keenly aware of the shortfall between the treaty's promises and the government's performance.

J. C. Richmond, a Taranaki settler, spoke for some, though not all, settlers when he looked forward to the treaty being over-ruled so 'Maori claims to the extensive bushlands would no longer be able to damp the ardour and cramp the energies of the industrious white man.' Comments like these often arose from irritation over land dealings. Richmond was later native minister.

The settlers take more power

In the 1850s settler society grew rapidly. The governing bodies which settlers wanted were set up under the 1852 Constitution Act. The right to vote was given to all males over twenty-one who had a freehold estate of a certain value. Since most Maori property was communal and unregistered, few Maori males qualified for the vote. The few who did participate in elections were resented by settlers.

When Governor Gore Browne arrived in 1855, therefore, he did not find the two races 'forming one people', as Grey's reports had led him to believe. He realised that Maori had no say in how the country was governed, despite their essential role in the economy. He decided to keep responsibility for Maori affairs himself. This did not work very well. Maori and settler interests were inextricably mixed. He still had to persuade a settler parliament to vote him the money to carry out Maori policy.

Browne also knew that many Maori communities were living beyond the boundaries of effective government authority. Little was being done to help them deal with new laws and regulations introduced by the provincial governments as well as the national government. At the same time chiefly authority was not getting the support that many Maori had expected from the treaty's guarantee.

Towards the end of the 1850s, as the Maori and European population drew even at about 60 000 each, the Maori people found that settler attitudes were changing. Many new colonists looked on the treaty as an unavoidable nuisance, a hangover from the colony's early days, which would have to be accepted – for a time at least.

Alfred Domett, an early Nelson settler, who admitted that he had 'an utter contempt' for the treaty. He thought that its land guarantee had been 'unwise'. During the months of the war in the Waikato in 1863, Domett was one of the major government leaders.

Tamati Ngapora, a chief noted for his caution and diplomacy, painted by Gottfried Lindauer. In the 1840s he asked Governor Grey for a law to strengthen chiefly authority so that it would benefit Maori and Pakeha. Grey rejected the suggestion.

Land selling increases

While Grey was governor he pushed ahead with land purchases. Under his chief land purchase commissioner, Donald McLean, procedures were worked out for negotiating sales at tribal meetings. If a meeting agreed to a sale, the purchase deed would often be signed by many of the tribe. Grey and McLean worked hard to overcome Maori reluctance to sell, sometimes using intense pressure to persuade chiefs, as Grey did in the Wairarapa, and sometimes dealing with only a few owners, as McLean began to do in the early 1850s. In Grey's governorship they succeeded in buying over a million hectares in the North Island, and over ten million hectares in the South Island.

Chiefs were often persuaded to accept ridiculously low purchase prices by government promises of schools, hospitals, and generous land reserves. But it was hard to hold the government to its promises. In the South Island, where land was bought for the Otago and Canterbury settlements, Maori leaders were rapidly disappointed. Appeals were made immediately to government officials. Tiramorehu was one who wrote repeatedly, as in 1849: 'This is but the start of our complaining to you. We shall never cease complaining to the white people who may hereafter come here.'

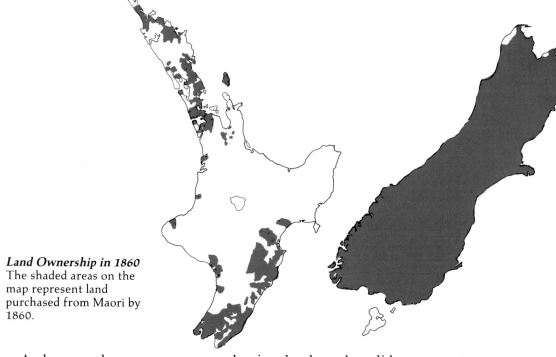

Land Ownership in 1860
The shaded areas on the map represent land purchased from Maori by 1860.

As long as the government was buying land, settlers did not see the treaty as too obstructive to the colony's development. When Maori owners refused to sell, however, it was a different matter. This happened in the 1850s, as tribal leaders began to realise how land negotiations were seriously threatening their authority.

A Maori King

The idea of setting up a Maori King to help the people was promoted by Tamihana Te Rauparaha and his cousin, Matene Te Whiwhi. In 1853 they travelled through central North Island districts, persuading tribes that a king would protect their lands and give the tribes unity. There was little Pakeha settlement in the central North Island and the two men thought that it should stay that way.

The idea of a veto on land sales caught on; so too did the wish for a king. A great meeting in South Taranaki in 1854 decided that land sales should end or at least be curtailed; and in 1858 Te Wherowhero was installed as the first Maori King.

The leaders of the King movement wanted to have Maori and Pakeha living in peace. Chiefs such as Wiremu Tamihana had thriving villages, busy with agriculture and trade. Wiremu Tamihana believed that the Maori King and the British Queen could work together like a partnership. In the treaty the mana of chieftainship and the mana of the Crown had both had a place.

Tamihana Te Rauparaha from Otaki. He was in England in 1851–52 and was presented to Queen Victoria. In the 1860s he was a successful sheepfarmer.

Wiremu Tamihana Tarapipipi built a model Christian village near Matamata in the 1840s. The village, called Peria, had clusters of houses for family groups, a large meeting house, a post office, a flour mill, and a schoolhouse with boarding accommodation for 100 students. There was a large church on one hill and a burial ground on another. The community had orchards and fields of wheat, maize, potatoes, and kumara which they traded in Auckland.

Governor Gore Browne with Mrs Harriet Browne, two of his children, and a member of his staff. Harriet Browne believed that her husband was right over Waitara and later wrote to defend his actions. In 1864 she wrote: 'This Waitara question is the skeleton of my life. I know my husband is an honest man.'

Officials thought differently. So did most Europeans. The King stood for Maori independence, and this irritated most officials and settlers who wanted the central North Island opened up for settlement.

Some thought that colonisation and the treaty were incompatible. Others held to the belief that the Crown was morally bound to uphold the treaty compact. Many, and finally most, Europeans thought that a war to assert British sovereignty was inevitable. A land sale in Taranaki became the test case.

The Waitara purchase

In 1859 a Te Ati Awa chief named Teira offered to sell the governor a piece of land at Waitara, north of New Plymouth. Other chiefs had an interest in the land, and usually the government would have negotiated with all parties before finalising the deal. But the government knew that some Te Ati Awa, including the senior chief Wiremu Kingi, were completely opposed to the sale. By accepting Teira's offer, the government aimed to break the opposition, to go against the wishes of an important chief and force the sale. This was a new way of dealing with Maori land ownership and was seen by some – Maori and Pakeha – as breaking the treaty's land guarantee. Taranaki settlers, however, saw the Waitara purchase as a test of the government's strength.

The governor and his advisers considered that the problem was not only about land but about the authority of the Crown to run the affairs of the country. Some argued that Teira had a right, as a British subject, to sell his land if he chose to. Communal ownership and chiefly authority were both at stake.

The sale went ahead; the deed of purchase was signed in February 1860. Surveyors went on to the land to mark it out. Shortly after, Kingi's people peacefully challenged them and disrupted their work. British troops were sent in to protect the surveyors. Fighting began and for a year utterly disrupted the lives of Maori and settlers in Taranaki.

The Kohimarama conference – July and August 1860

Governor Browne knew that Maori would criticise him for his policy on the Waitara land purchase. So he decided to rally as much Maori support as possible. To do this, he held a large gathering of chiefs at Mission Bay in Auckland. It became known as the Kohimarama conference. The government had not made such an effort to sound out Maori opinion before; the conference was the most representative and important Maori gathering ever held. Some of the chiefs had signed the treaty in 1840. All were related to someone who had signed. The only leaders absent were from Taranaki and some from Waikato.

Wiremu Kingi Te Rangitake. Before the Taranaki wars Wiremu Kingi had written to the governor and the governor's chief land purchase agent, Donald McLean, about the lands the tribe wanted to retain, including Waitara: 'These are the lands we will not give up, for we would be like sea birds perched on a rock: when the tide flows, the rock is covered by the sea and the birds have to fly off, because there is no place for them to rest.' After the wars Wiremu Kingi lived in inland Taranaki until his death in 1882.

An enterprise most difficult

Both Sir William Martin, the retired Chief Justice, and Lady Mary, his wife, were deeply upset by the events in Taranaki. Here is an excerpt from a book Sir William Martin wrote about the situation:

> Here in New Zealand our nation has engaged in an enterprise most difficult, yet also most noble and worthy of England. We have undertaken to acquire these islands for the Crown and for our race, without violence and without fraud, and so that the Native people, instead of being destroyed, should be protected and civilised. We have convenanted with these people, and assured to them the full privileges of subjects of the Crown. To this undertaking the faith of the nation is pledged. By these means we secured a peaceable entrance for the Queen's authority into the country, and have in consequence gradually gained a firm hold upon it. The compact is binding irrevocably. We cannot repudiate it so long as we retain the benefit which we obtained by it.

Two years before Waitara, Lady Mary Martin travelled through the Waikato. Later she wrote of her journey:

> Our path lay across a wide plain, and our eyes were gladdened on all sides by sights of peaceful industry. For miles we saw one great wheat field . . . . Carts were driven to and from the mill by their native owners, women sat under trees sewing flour bags and babies swarmed around . . . We little dreamed that in ten years the peaceful industry of the whole district would cease and the land become a desert through our unhappy war.

Mary Martin, wife of the Chief Justice, like many other settlers was opposed to war as a way of overcoming difficulties.

Governor Browne opened the conference by talking about the treaty of Waitangi. He repeated the pledges made by the Crown and by chiefs. But he was careful not to stress the view that Maori had handed over their sovereignty (which was again translated just as kawanatanga or government).

His explanation of the second article was very important indeed. It spelt out (as the treaty in Maori had not) that Maori rights to forests and fisheries, as well as lands, were guaranteed. They had always been covered by the treaty in English, but the governor's words confirmed this beyond any doubt. However, he did not speak of te tino rangatiratanga (rights of chieftainship), but just of a guarantee of possession.

The chiefs speak

We know what was said by chiefs at the meeting because we can read the speeches in English and in Maori. Each chief checked his speech for accuracy before it was printed. They show that many of the chiefs had not known in 1840 what signing the treaty would mean to them. Some had found out only when British authority extended into their tribal area and they had to start obeying a new set of laws.

'It is true I received one blanket,' said one chief from Wellington. 'I did not understand what was meant by it; it was given to me without any explanation.'

Other chiefs wondered if the treaty was still in force when it had been broken by the spilling of blood – the Wairau, the northern war, and the fighting in Taranaki.

Nga Puhi leaders, however, had a very definite understanding of the treaty as a sacred covenant, unifying Maori with Maori, and Maori with Pakeha.

Some chiefs realised that the governor might make treaty guarantees conditional on all Maori accepting government authority. Tamati Waka Nene urged chiefs to consider this carefully: 'I am not accepting the Pakeha for myself alone, but for the whole of us.' He reminded them that, though many of them were old enemies, thanks to Christianity brought by the English, 'we are able to meet together this day, under one roof . . . I say, I know no Sovereign but the Queen . . . I am walking by the side of the Pakeha.'

At the final conference session, chiefs resolved that they were 'pledged to each other to do nothing inconsistent with their declared recognition of the Queen's sovereignty, and of the union of the two races'. They also promised to have nothing to do with anything that might break this covenant they had 'solemnly entered into'.

The pledge became known as the Kohimarama covenant, and, with the conference as a whole, was as important to Maori understanding of the Treaty of Waitangi as the meetings to sign the treaty in 1840. The covenant was like a new, or renewed, commitment to the treaty as a very sacred deed. Many northern chiefs had always seen it this way, but now the idea was shared by other chiefs from all over the country, including tribes who had not signed in 1840.

Government mana and Maori mana
The most important idea retained by Maori leaders from the conference was that Maori mana had been guaranteed. Partly this was because the governor and the chairman Donald McLean had stressed this in their explanations of the treaty. But it was also because the conference itself was a recognition of rangatiratanga. Chiefs had expressed their dissatisfaction

Paora Tuhaere of Ngati Whatua. He complained that most tribes had not been represented at the 1840 meeting at Waitangi. 'But this conference,' he said, 'is . . . the real treaty upon which the sovereignty of the Queen will hang because here are assembled chiefs from every quarter . . . to discuss questions and to seek out a path.'

Mete Kingi of Wanganui attended the Kohimarama conference. He was the first member for Western Maori in the House of Representatives from 1868 to 1870.

over the unequal participation of Maori in law and government. They petitioned the governor to make the conference a permanent institution. The government agreed and promised to reconvene the assembly in 1861.

Parakaia of Ngati Raukawa expressed his pleasure at the possibility of greater participation. 'Now, perhaps, for the first time, shall I fully enter into the arrangements of the English Government, and now, perhaps, for the first time, will what I have to say be heard.'

But Browne did not really achieve what he had hoped from the conference. He failed to get support from the chiefs over his Waitara policy and his condemnation of the King movement. Many chiefs were critical of the government's failure to investigate Waitara carefully. They thought that the government should have referred the dispute to mediation by appointed Maori leaders.

> ### The New Zealand Wars
> The New Zealand Wars were a series of engagements which steadily expanded the area of fighting. Starting as moves against Taranaki and Waikato, they had, by the end of the 1860s, involved almost all North Island districts, directly or indirectly. British troops, whose numbers were steadily built up to 18 000 at peak, were joined by colonial troops and by Maori forces prepared to fight on the Queen's side. Set-piece battles in the Waikato and at Tauranga gave way to guerrilla warfare in Taranaki and on the East Coast.

The King movement was a more difficult problem for some chiefs. They were willing to accept the Queen's authority in its protective sense. But they were reluctant to admit that the authority of a chief like the King could not sit alongside the Queen's authority. After all, the concept of a shared authority or mana, which the treaty seemed to allow for, was applicable to all chiefs and not just to the King.

Browne and the King movement

In the first half of 1861 the government seemed to be drifting towards a showdown on the question of sovereignty. Some Waikato had become involved in the Taranaki fighting. The first King, Te Wherowhero, had died. His son, Tawhiao, had become the second King. The King movement looked as if it would last. The governor was even more determined that something should be done about it.

About this time, there were strong rumours going around that Governor Browne was bent on depriving Maori of their land, and that he was determined to destroy chiefly influence. In March 1861, Browne wrote in the *Maori Messenger* to deny this. He repeated the second article of the treaty. But in May he sent a proclamation to the Waikato tribes accusing them of violating the treaty. He demanded 'submission without reserve to the Queen's sovereignty and the authority of the Law'.

Wiremu Tamihana wrote a thoughtful reply pointing out the understanding of the treaty that the King's closest advisers had always had: that there was a place for an independent Maori leadership in co-operation with the Queen's sovereignty or mana. Frederick Weld, the government minister responsible for Maori affairs, read such a letter as a statement of 'Maori nationality' or independence. He was convinced, as were some other government people, that force was needed to impose European superiority on native races.

Tawhiao, who became King when Te Wherowhero died in 1860. Under Tawhiao the King movement kept growing. After the wars he remained King until his death in 1894.

Razor Back Hill on the road to the Waikato.

Wars of sovereignty

War did come, despite efforts by many Maori and Europeans to avoid it. With the government and the King movement holding different views of sovereign rights, a meeting of minds was near impossible. Grey returned as governor in November 1861 and tried to negotiate. At the same time he had a military road built from Auckland into the Waikato. The Maori were highly suspicious of his plans. But the King movement tried, in January 1863, to get his agreement to their terms, based on the treaty's guarantee of Maori mana over lands, forests and fisheries. The King's control in the Waikato was to be respected. The governor's road-making – 'cutting the land's backbone' – was to stop at the Mangatawhiri stream. And no armed steamers (then being built) were to be allowed up the Waikato river.

Grey was evasive, and for some months a paper war of articles and reports in newspapers kept Maori and settlers on tenterhooks. Finally, when war broke out again in Taranaki, Grey and the government decided to strike a blow at Waikato. On 12 July British troops crossed over the Mangatawhiri stream, and the wars began in earnest. A proclamation, issued too late to reach the Waikato, warned the King's supporters that those who 'rebelled' would have their lands confiscated.

Women fought in the 1860s wars and some died. This is Heni Te Kirikaramu with a flag she made when fighting with the King's forces. Later she fought on the government side with Te Arawa troops.

British withdrawal

As the fighting dragged on into the mid 1860s, British troops and their officers came to the conclusion that they were fighting a war for land on behalf of settlers, against an enemy that the troops respected. Many settlers, too, were deeply disturbed that two races, who had aimed to make a new nation together, had ended up fighting.

The fighting drew to an untidy conclusion at the end of the 1860s. In 1870 the last British troops left, and the British government determined to pour no more money into New Zealand. The colonial government, now fully responsible for the Maori people, was more prepared to state bluntly that

Confiscated Lands 1864–67
The New Zealand Settlements Act authorised the confiscation of lands from those in 'rebellion' in any district of New Zealand. The shaded areas on the map show the lands confiscated. Some were later returned.

the Maori people had signed away the mana of the country in 1840.

The Maori people were well aware of the diminishing of their mana in the 1860s. But they did not accept that agreeing to British sovereignty meant giving up altogether the mana of chieftainship. For them, this was a new interpretation of the treaty of Waitangi.

It was some time before Maori leaders fully realised that responsibility for their affairs had been transferred from the British to the New Zealand government. They could hardly believe that the Queen and her British parliament had washed their hands of the Waitangi covenant. But they had.

A group of prisoners, captured at Weraroa pa at Waitotara in Taranaki, on the prison hulk in Wellington Harbour.

The Colonial Government Takes Charge

1870–1900

The wars finally ended around 1870. The government could claim a victory on the battlefield, even though a very narrow one. Perhaps because of this, European attitudes to the treaty were tougher. Politicians and officials talked little of its benefits. They disparaged it, or insisted that it committed the Maori people to obey the law.

To the thousands of settlers who began arriving in the government's immigration and development schemes, the treaty was past history. The Maori population seemed to be declining steadily; a country with few Maori survivors seemed highly likely.

Yet the treaty could not be completely ignored. The government still had to deal with Maori land, and sometimes with fisheries now too. As government authority and Pakeha settlement reached out to the most remote Maori villages, the treaty became more important than ever to the Maori people.

The Native Land Court

In 1865 the Native Land Court was set up. Its business was to find out who owned Maori land and to grant the owners a certificate of title so that Maori land could come under the same law as Pakeha-owned land. The court recognised owners as those who had rights to land in 1840, the year of the signing of the treaty. Land could be sold to settlers only after it had been through the court. The costs of taking claims to court, of getting land surveyed, and other expenses often got Maori leaders heavily into debt. To repay loans they had to sell land.

Through confiscation of land after the wars about 800 000 hectares of Maori land was seized, but the court's work led

onald McLean,
uperintendent of Hawke's
ay, meeting with Maori to
urchase Wairoa, 1865.

Maori population trends		
Census year	Maori population	Total population
1874	47 330	344 984
1881	46 141	534 030
1891	44 177	668 632
1901	45 549	815 862
1911	52 723	1 058 312
1921	56 987	1 271 668
1936	82 326	1 573 812
1945	98 744	1 702 330
1956	137 151	2 174 062
1966	201 159	2 676 919
1976	270 035	3 129 383
1986	405 309	3 307 084

These figures were derived from census returns.

The MP for Southern
Maori, Henare Uru,
attending a native land
court sitting early in the
twentieth century at
Temuka.

to far more land being lost and affected all tribes. By 1892 the Maori people owned only a little over a third of the North Island, about 4.5 million hectares, of which a quarter was leased to Pakeha. Another million hectares was sold by around 1900 and the loss continued until at least 1921. Numerous

Report on land

In 1891 a royal commission examining the administration of Maori land law exposed unscrupulous fraud in a process that was little more than legalised land-grabbing. In the South Island, Maori had only a few reserves totalling less than 100 000 hectares.

Native Land Court

Numerous witnesses bear testimony to the gradual deterioration of the Native Land Court. It takes a longer time now to hear a case than formerly. Its fees and charges are greatly in excess of what they were. Its adjournments and postponements are more frequent and inconvenient. The applications for rehearings are greatly increased. It has gradually lost every characteristic of a Native Court, and has become entirely European – as Hone Peeti said, 'only the name remaining.' It has brought into existence a regular system of concocting false claims, by which the real owners are often driven out, and their land given to clever rogues of their own race. It no longer visits the land, nor guides and advises the Natives in friendly settlements. Its demand for excessive daily fees is so imperious that Natives not able to pay are refused a hearing, and thus in many cases the real owners are compelled to stand by and see their land given to strangers. Its decisions are never final. Even after years of occupation under a certificate, Crown grant, or transfer title, the occupier is liable to litigation, ejectment, and ruin owing to the numerous methods available for setting them at nought, or, at any rate, interfering with them through the ever varying conditions of the law.

So complete has the confusion both in law and practice become that lawyers of high standing and extensive practice have testified on oath that if the Legislature had desired to create a state of confusion and anarchy in Native-land titles it could not have hoped to be more successful than it has been. Were it not that the facts are vouched upon the testimony of men whose character is above suspicion and whose knowledge is undoubted, it would be well-nigh impossible to believe that a state of such disorder could exist.

acts of parliament and two major government commissions of enquiry did not halt this.

These kinds of problems over land divided Maori communities against themselves and were utterly demoralising. Leaders used the country's law courts as well as the land court to try to settle their difficulties. In the 1880s they presented hundreds of petitions to parliament. Maori were using their rights as British subjects to claim justice, but the

Seafood of all kinds has always been relished by Maori. Here are Auntie Neta and Auntie Sally eating kina (sea eggs) at Manukorihi Marae in Taranaki.

This piharau (lamprey eel), is a delicacy much prized by Maori.

Aila Taylor. In 1982 he asked the Waitangi Tribunal to protect Te Ati Awa reefs in north Taranaki from sewage and industrial waste.

government and the courts found many reasons why Maori complaints could not be satisfied. One reason was that the treaty had not been made part of any law passed by parliament; so the courts did not recognise it. In 1877 Chief Justice James Prendergast declared it a legal 'nullity'.

From 1867 there were four Maori members of parliament to represent the Maori people. They could not persuade a majority of European members that injustices of various kinds should be attended to. From the end of the wars the various governments saw development of the country as more important than recognition of Maori rights.

Fisheries and food-gathering rights

For about twenty years after 1840 fishing rights, confirmed by the treaty, were given some recognition by the government,

> ### Hori Ngatai's words to John Ballance
> 'Now, with regard to the land below high water mark immediately in front of where I live, I consider that this is part and parcel of my own land . . . part of my own garden . . . [As for] the fishing-grounds inside the Tauranga Harbour [my] mana over these places has never been taken away. I have always held authority over these fishing-places and preserved them; and no tribe is allowed to come here and fish without my consent being given. But now . . . people [Europeans] . . . are constantly here whenever they like to fish. I ask that our . . . authority over these fishing-grounds may be upheld . . .'

Hori Ngatai.

although there was no set policy. People writing about Maori life both before and after 1840 talked about the importance of fisheries of all kinds to the Maori, both for food and for trade. Certain fishing grounds were often exclusively used by particular hapu. Others could use them, perhaps, but only with permission. Sometimes rights could be transferred.

The Maori people guarded fishing grounds with as much care as they did their land. But the supplies of fish were so extensive in New Zealand that it was only as settlement expanded that tensions between Maori and Pakeha developed.

In 1855 the Resident Magistrate at Kaipara, north of Auckland, wrote to Attorney General William Swainson:

> On the West Coast between high and low water marks, there exists . . . a bed of toheroa. This fishery is highly valued by the natives. At present, the value of the fishery as . . . food has been discovered by the Europeans, and large quantities are carried [away] for the use of the workmen on the European stations.

Ngati Whatua, the local tribe, were asking for a rental to be paid for such use; but the Europeans were claiming that the land below high water mark was the property of the Crown. Swainson was not too sure how to handle the complaint. But in 1872 a ruling by another attorney general agreed with the Europeans' claim. It was one step of many which gradually whittled away recognition of Maori fishing rights. By 1910 the Crown was claiming that it had absolute ownership of beds of lakes too.

Some acknowledgement of Maori rights was made under an 1877 Fisheries Act which dealt with salt and fresh water fisheries:

> Nothing in this Act contained shall be deemed to repeal, alter, or affect any of the provisions of the Treaty of Waitangi, or to take away, annul, or abridge any of the rights of the aboriginal natives to any fishery secured to them thereunder.

In practice it did not make Maori fishing rights secure under law. Some special enactment or provision was needed before Maori rights could be asserted.

Maori protests

From the 1860s Maori began to battle for fishing rights offshore, in foreshores, lakes, rivers, and harbours. For example, Maori leaders and government officers drew the government's attention to the depletion of pipi beds in the Manukau Harbour and oyster beds in the Bay of Islands. James Mackay reported on rights, as he saw them in 1869:

> The Natives occasionally exercise certain privileges or rights over tidal lands. They are not considered as the common property of all Natives in the Colony; but certain hapus or tribes have the right to fish over one mud flat and other Natives over another. Sometimes even this goes so far as to give certain rights out at sea. For instance, at Katikati Harbour, one tribe of Natives have a right to fish within the line of tide-rip; another tribe of Natives have the right to fish outside the tide-rip.

In 1877 H.K. Taiaroa, the member for Southern Maori, wanted to know by what authority Europeans were 'plundering all the oysters and fish' from the Mangahoe Inlet in Otago and selling them in Dunedin. When John Ballance, then minister of native affairs, visited Tauranga in 1885, Ngai Te Rangi leader Hori Ngatai asserted publicly Maori rights to the foreshore and sea bed against the government's claim that the Crown owned them.

Wairarapa Lakes – a conflict of interests

Sometimes a battle for a fishery right would go on for years, such as in the Wairarapa Lakes. The two lakes were a very important source of food to local Maori. Eels were caught in large numbers at the shingle bar which dammed the seaward

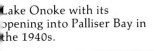
Lake Onoke with its opening into Palliser Bay in the 1940s.

end of the lower lake. Dried eels were given away as gifts or were exchanged with other tribes for preserved birds and shellfish.

In 1853 the government purchased some adjacent land and recognised Maori fishing rights. But in the 1860s local settlers pressured the government to open the shingle bar so the lands surrounding the lakes would not be flooded. Piripi Te Maari, who was himself a successful farmer in the area, together with others appealed to the government to uphold the original agreement. Settlers wanted the government to buy the lakes and quash Maori rights.

The struggle continued through the 1870s, 1880s and 1890s. Te Maari agreed to a compromise in 1886: the lake's bar would be opened ten months of the year and only closed during the height of the fishing season in February and March. The Ruamahanga River Board objected and twice tried to force the bar open. Te Maari petitioned the government twice, secured a commission of enquiry (which was non-committal), took a case to the Court of Appeal (it was dismissed), threatened to go to the Privy Council, and finally, in 1895, secured a favourable decision from the government that the lakes' owners should receive compensation for lost rights. The Crown gave the owners land in distant Mangakino.

A river board team, sent with shovels to open the bar of Lake Onoke. Such teams were part of the running battle between local settlers and Maori wishing to maintain their eel fishery.

Problems common to all tribes

The difficulties experienced by Wairarapa Maori were similar to those elsewhere and they were to continue into the twentieth century. In the South Island, in 1868, land to give access to fisheries was set aside – 212 acres (80 hectares) in Canterbury and 112 acres (45 hectares) in Otago – but the 1891 commission on South Island land reported:

> The Natives at Waitaki . . . are very badly off for food supplies . . . and, to make matters more trying they cannot fish in the Waitaki for eels or whitebait, owing to that river being stocked with imported fish. . . . The natives [at Lake Ellesmere] . . . are gradually being deprived of all their former privileges . . . through the drainage of the land, as well as through all the rivers, lakes, and lagoons being stocked with imported fish.

weirs on the Wanganui
er, 1924. When a royal
mmission on claims
ating to the Wanganui
er reported in 1950, it
d that the Maori Land
urt had found that
aori eel weirs and other
h traps on the river had
en 'indiscriminately . . .
stroyed or done away
h to provide a passage
river steamers. Any
otest of the unfortunate
ople who owned the eel-
irs remained unheeded.'
1882 compensation had
en paid to allow
vigation of the Patea
er.

In 1903, T. Parata, the Member for Southern Maori, claimed that,

> . . . along the coast of Otago, and right up to Akaroa, there are a number of fishing grounds that have been handed down to the Maoris by their ancestors, but have been overrun and made use of by everybody, including Europeans, in recent years. I do not object to the Europeans fishing at these places, but these reefs should be to some extent protected for the benefit of the Maoris; and there are other parts of the sea which are available for European fishermen to make use of.

Protests continued as Maori leaders searched for ways of making government and public listen.

Searching into the treaty

There were plenty of reasons, apart from land and fishery problems, why the Maori people began to look more closely at the treaty of Waitangi in the years after the wars. The steady expansion of settlement, accompanied by road-making, drainage, and other kinds of works brought the most remote Maori communities under the control of local and national government. Maori communities with limited access to money found it nearly impossible to meet demands for rates to pay for local government and roads. Rates, like a tax levied on dogs from 1880, were seen as infringing individual rights.

It was clear to many Maori that the treaty's protection was very limited. It had no power, for instance, against the Public Works Acts of 1864 and 1876, which allowed land to be taken compulsorily for public development (nor against later acts). Court decisions, shady dealings and legislation were all playing a part in undermining the treaty's guarantees.

These are Ngati Maniapoto chiefs of the King Country in about 1884. Rewi, the great fighting chief, is at the left rear.

The King Country

In 1865 and 1866 Wiremu Tamihana petitioned the government for an inquiry into the Waikato war and a return of the confiscated land. The government ignored him. Tawhiao then withdrew behind the aukati, the confiscation line. The region under his jurisdiction – about 11 000 square kilometres – became known as the King Country. Europeans were warned to stay out.

Runanga and conferences

In a series of runanga (very large gatherings) Maori discussed ways of mending tribal ties damaged in the wars, of coming to terms with the Pakeha world, and of forcing the government to uphold the treaty. Each tribe had its own special concerns, but they shared a common bond in the treaty and in the relationship they understood it had laid with the government. The conferences that were most concerned with treaty rights met at Auckland and at Waitangi.

Meetings at Orakei

Paora Tuhaere of Ngati Whatua had waited in vain for the government to reconvene the Kohimarama conference. So, in March 1879, he held a conference at Orakei, attended by about 300 chiefs. For almost half of the nine-day gathering he kept discussion centred on the treaty and its interpretation.

In December 1878 Rewi made his peace with George Grey, then premier of New Zealand, at a great hui at Waitara, shown here. Note the wall of food kits, topped by pigs. It was customary to collect food in this way and then distribute it to guests.

The treaty was read out and so was Governor Browne's explanation given at the 1860 conference.

People at the conference saw the treaty as a covenant of peace and unity between tribes and between Maori and Pakeha. But, as Tuhaere noted, the Maori people were disillusioned with government policy. They felt that the Queen's protection had passed away.

> That Treaty of Waitangi left the rights of the soil with the Maori chiefs . . . [The Queen] left the fisheries to the Maoris . . . . She also left us the places where the pipis, mussels, and oysters, and other shellfish are collected . . . Let us see whether the stipulations made in the Treaty of Waitangi are still in force or not.

The conference ended with resolutions which asserted the mana of the Maori people 'over fishing grounds and deep water shark', and 'over flounder and eel fisheries', and 'over sandbanks of pipi, rock oysters, mussels, paua, kina and scallops'.

Tuhaere held further conferences in 1880 and 1881. Those attending recalled that in 1835 elders in the north had formed a confederation and had decided to hold annual runanga where chiefs would lay down laws for New Zealand. Since the treaty had recognised the confederation and confirmed rangatiratanga, Maori leaders felt they were entitled to exercise

65

The meeting in progress, chaired by Tuhaere, with a Pakeha interpreter and reporter below him. Hirini Taiwhanga is the speaker.

their rights by holding conferences or parliaments. At the same time they were anxious that the idea of the two races being one people – so often expressed by officials – would not be forgotten. They could see that government policies in the 1880s were dividing them.

Meetings at Waitangi

The first of the Nga Puhi parliaments opened in March 1881 at Te Tii marae, Waitangi; over 3,000 attended. Northern leaders called for a Maori parliament to weld the Maori people into a united body to fight for treaty rights. They wanted to be associated with the government, but on Maori terms; they were not looking for separation.

The government was not interested in their request, and, although parliaments at Waitangi were held each year through the 1880s, Maori leaders found it impossible to influence government policy.

Petitioning the Queen

Maori leaders now turned to England, to Queen Victoria with whom the treaty had been made. She was the 'great mother' who had offered her protection in 1840. In the 1880s, two deputations took petitions to England. But the British government could not let the Queen receive such delegations. Her ministers, after consulting with the New Zealand government, dealt with the Maori leaders and insisted that only the New Zealand government could handle Maori

Maihi Paraone Kawiti was one of the main organisers of the meetings at Waitangi in the 1880s. He was the son of Kawiti who had challenged British sovereignty in the 1840s. In 1858 he and a group of warriors who had fought in the war re-erected the flagstaff on Russell hill.

1882 petition to the Queen

The petitioners appealed to the Queen to appoint a 'Royal English Commission' to investigate and rectify laws that contravened the treaty, and asked that permission be given to establish a Maori parliament which would restrain the New Zealand government in its endeavours to set aside the treaty.

The petition recounted at length the confiscations, the native land court, local body taxes and government ill-treatment of Te Whiti. It listed legislative acts and ordinances that were said to be 'against the principles contained in the treaty'. It also outlined the history of Pakeha–Maori strife over land. The establishment of the King movement was described as a legitimate act to protect Maori lands in accordance with the treaty's provisions.

matters. It was a great disappointment to the many tribes all over New Zealand who had placed great hopes in the appeals.

Kotahitanga

Plans were now made for a Maori parliament that would involve all tribes, coming together in the spirit of kotahitanga – unity or oneness. Its business would be to sort out Maori needs and present them as effectively as possible to the Wellington parliament. The first session met at Waipatu, near Hastings, in 1892, and annual parliaments were held until 1902.

The Maori members of the Wellington parliament took part in the Maori parliament sessions too. But the government simply ignored the advice and requests of the Maori parliament and refused to recognise it. Without any authority from the Crown, the Maori parliaments were powerless. Although they stopped meeting, the ideas and aims of Kotahitanga have continued to the present time.

Just as the Kotahitanga parliaments were being planned in 1890, New Zealand was celebrating its fiftieth anniversary as a British colony. People's minds turned back to the early years, but not so much to the treaty as to the arrival of the first settler ships in Wellington, and to the coming of Hobson on 29 January 1840 (which became the official anniversary day). It showed how much Pakeha New Zealanders had forgotten the treaty.

Two Peoples – One Nation
The Twentieth Century

For the Maori people in the new century, the treaty remained central to their struggle to gain rights from the government. They kept hoping that official attitudes to the treaty might change. After all, elections sometimes brought changes of government, and in time new politicians might listen to Maori voices.

Sometimes they did. In 1900 parliament passed two acts which were meant to give some power to Maori in organising their own affairs. The Native Councils Act set up committees of elders in Maori communities. It gave them certain legal powers to deal with such things as health and education of their people. But the committees – the government's alternative to the Maori parliaments – were not widely accepted by Maori. Committee powers were very limited, and they were not given enough money to carry out their tasks adequately.

Land loss continues

The Native Lands Administration Act set up land councils with Maori members in the majority to administer leasing of Maori land. But little was made available. In 1905 the government replaced the councils with Pakeha-dominated native land boards, which had the power to take Maori land into their control compulsorily. This made it easier for land to be opened up for Pakeha settlement at the very time that many Maori people were beginning to farm their land successfully.

At the same time, well-educated young men, collectively known as the Young Maori Party, were committed to making parliament and government departments work for the good of their people. One of them, Apirana Ngata, entered parliament in 1905. In 1907, Ngata was appointed with Sir Robert

Stout to investigate Maori land questions. They predicted that the Maori would become an impoverished, landless people unless government policy changed.

The Native Land Act of 1909 adopted many of their suggestions. For example, £50,000 was set aside for Maori land development. But a similar amount was made available to buy Maori land. One section of the act also allowed for Maori land to be taken for roads and railways with no compensation paid.

Between 1911 and 1920 the Maori people lost half of their remaining land; of the other half, some was leased to Pakeha and some was unsuitable for farming.

Maori who wanted to farm faced a real problem in securing loan money to develop their land. Maori land, if the land court had not investigated its ownership, had no European title that a loan agency required before lending money. If the land did have European title, it might have hundreds of owners who might not all agree on its use. Loan agencies were reluctant to lend in such a case.

In 1926, the native land boards were authorised to advance money for development, using the land as security even if the title was undecided. Ngata was behind this. In 1928, as minister of native affairs, he persuaded the government to pass an act to allow Maori farmers to develop their land. He found ways of overcoming all sorts of handicaps and, by 1934, many thousands of hectares were under development. The land was providing a living for about 18,000 Maori by 1937.

Maori soldiers taking a break while working on improving the trenches near Gommecourt in France, July 1918. In World War I tribal and religious leaders such as Te Puea, Te Rata, and Rua Kenana urged neutrality on their followers. But other leaders – professional men and MPs such as Maui Pomare and Apirana Ngata – wanted Maori to go to the war to show they were as capable as Europeans. Several contingents of volunteer Maori Pioneers went before June 1917 when Maori became liable for conscription. At that stage a fighting unit, which became known as the Maori Battalion, was formed. Some Waikato Maori were gaoled for resisting conscription.

Failure and success

During this period, the treaty was a major topic of discussion on marae, especially after the First World War. One issue was a matter of failure on the government's part. As British subjects, Maori soldiers did their part in the war. They had fought valiantly and many had been killed. When war ended the government helped Pakeha soldiers to re-establish themselves in civilian life, through trade training and farm schemes, but it did not do the same for Maori.

On the other hand, the government finally agreed that compensation should be paid to Te Arawa tribe for fishing and burial rights in the Rotorua lakes. In 1926 a similar agreement was reached with Ngati Tuwharetoa over their rights to Lake Taupo and adjoining streams.

Naturally these moves created great interest in Maori communities. For years, individuals and groups had tried, unsuccessfully, to have fishing rights of various kinds made secure. These agreements on lakes raised Maori hopes, not only about fishing rights but about land and the matter of Maori authority in general.

F. A. Bennett, the first Maori bishop, wrote an appeal in 1912 for Te Arawa rights to their lakes.

T.W. Ratana, the founder of the Ratana church (centre picture). In 1918 Ratana believed he had a special mission to unite the Maori people. He built a temple at Ratana pa, near Wanganui, and within a few years his church had more than 20 000 members. Big gatherings are still held at the pa and the faith is strong.

With Ratana are the men who were all to become MPs by 1943. Left (seated), H.T. Ratana; right (seated), E.T. Tirikatene; left (standing), P.K. Paikea; right (standing), T. Omana.

Eruera Tirikatene and his daughter Whetu in 1959. As the first Ratana MP he presented a petition to parliament, containing over 30 000 signatures, asking for statutory recognition of the treaty. The government responded in 1945 by printing the treaty and asking that copies be hung in every school and meeting house in the country.

New political parties and Maori aspirations

In the 1920s the Ratana church established itself as a political movement. Its main aim was to have the treaty 'ratified' as part of the law of the land. The treaty would then have to be recognised by the government and the courts. From the 1943 election, all four Maori seats were held by Ratana members, pledged to promote the treaty. This success meant that appeals over treaty rights would continue and would be made at national level.

As important perhaps was the alliance established between the Ratana movement and the Labour Party when it became the government in 1935. It ensured that the treaty would become a more important part of the political scene than it had been for many years. Ratana members worked hard to implement Labour's promises on the treaty, for a long time with little result. But they kept alive the objective of building the treaty into the law.

The gift of Waitangi

In May 1932 Busby's house at Waitangi was gifted to the nation by the governor general, Lord Bledisloe, and his wife; over 2000 acres (800 hectares) of land were part of the gift. The Bledisloes launched an appeal to develop the property as a 'national memorial'. These actions, more than any other single factor, led to renewed Pakeha interest in the treaty and the 1840 events. The development of the site encouraged more Maori interest too.

To celebrate the gift, a great hui at Te Tii, hosted by Nga Puhi, was held in February 1934. A second ceremony was

held at the treaty house where a flagpole had been erected on the spot where the treaty had been signed. Some 10,000 people came from all over New Zealand. It was exactly a hundred years since Britain's acknowledgement of Maori sovereignty. A replica of the flag chosen on that occasion was flown along with the Union Jack.

Te Tii marae at Waitangi in 1934 when the great hui was held to celebrate the gift of the property where the treaty was signed. The treaty house stands across the bridge among the trees.

The 1940 centennial

In 1940 another very large gathering was held at Waitangi to mark the country's centennial. The government was determined that it would be a great demonstration of national pride and unity. Thanks to the Bledisloes' gift, national attention was drawn to Waitangi and the treaty as it had not been in 1890. Newspapers talked of Waitangi as the 'cradle of the nation', and the treaty as the 'Magna Carta' and the 'foundation of nationhood' – expressions which, like the style of celebrations, set a pattern that would be repeated for years.

The Maori people did not support the 1940 event as they had the earlier one. Although the Labour government had poured more money into Maori affairs after 1935, especially into the land development begun by Ngata, many Maori felt an insensitivity to Maori matters in government circles. They were also disappointed in Labour's failure to honour promises. Many – especially Waikato and Taranaki – still felt sore that the injustices of the nineteenth century had not been settled. Others, like Ngai Tahu of the South Island, reminded

Apirana Ngata leading members of the Maori Battalion in a haka in front of the whare runanga on the Waitangi treaty house ground at the 1940 centennial celebrations. Ngata, MP for Eastern Maori from 1905 to 1943, wielded enormous influence among Maori during this period. He knew how much Maori energy could be spent in

This 30-metre long canoe was launched at Waitangi in 1940. There was a re-enactment of the treaty signing and speakers made much of the unity of Maori and Pakeha.

trying to get satisfaction for treaty-related issues. So, in 1922, he wrote an explanation of the treaty, in an attempt to get Maori to accept the government's understanding of rights of sovereignty and chiefly authority. In 1940, however, he asked the Labour government to settle grievances so that Maori could 'close their eyes to the past'.

the government that they were still waiting for settlement of some claims which had been officially recognised since the 1850s.

The Second World War and after

During the war the Maori people showed their ability at home and abroad. A special Maori War Effort Organisation worked under Maori leadership. Tribal committees across the country recruited Maori soldiers, supplied 'manpower' for essential jobs, and raised funds for war work. A Maori Battalion fought with distinction in some of the hardest battles of the war and suffered heavy casualties.

Maori hoped that their effort would lead, in peacetime, to more Maori control of their own affairs and to greater participation in government decision-making. But they were disappointed. Tribal committees were brought under a Maori Affairs Department that was dominated by Pakeha. This, and the setting up of a New Zealand Maori Council in 1962, were not the answer to Maori requests for a genuine sharing of power and authority.

After the war successive governments failed to meet Maori requests and needs. The first Labour government, for example, assisted the Maori people greatly by its policies aimed at giving everyone a decent standard of living. They also made special efforts for Maori in housing, education, and health. But the problems created by previous government actions were not fully appreciated and sometimes the remedies were not entirely appropriate. Pouring money into land development took care of only a proportion of the Maori population. For the rest, the government began to work out trade and other training only in the late 1940s. In the 1950s education policies were still stressing the need to make Maori children 'good farmers and good farmers' wives', when census figures showed that Maori were moving to the towns and cities at an increasing rate.

Waitangi Day

The second Labour government brought in the Waitangi Day Act in 1960. This declared that 6 February would be 'a national day of thanksgiving in commemoration of the signing' of the treaty. But the Maori MPs' request that it be a public holiday was defeated, and the act caused barely a ripple on the national scene. Waitangi Day remained mainly a northern affair.

Yet public interest was slowly growing. The trust board worked hard to promote the property; from 1950 a government

In the 1970s the Labour government tried to encourage pride in nationhood through creating new traditions. At one Waitangi ceremony Norman Kirk invited a young Maori boy to walk with him to the rostrum for the prime minister's speech.

department shared in the task of its maintenance and development. From brief ceremonies there on 6 February, the scope of the event began to develop and the style of ceremony took shape. The governor general and top government people began to attend. Speeches stressed the legendary good relations between Maori and Pakeha. Speechmakers seemed ignorant of the irritations and impediments affecting Maori communities. It was the beginning of a new wave of Maori protest.

Various laws were passed during the 1950s and 1960s that disregarded Maori values relating to land and were seen by Maori leaders as contravening the treaty. Maori were no longer prepared to stay silent about such things. They sensed that behind this legislation lay a strong Pakeha urge to absorb any separate Maori identity, that Hobson's 'one people' meant an all-Pakeha people, some more brown than others perhaps.

Through the 1960s and 1970s there was increasing Pakeha and Maori interest in Waitangi and the treaty; but the focus for each race was different. Pakeha were interested in the treaty as part of the country's history. Maori activity was directed towards securing a national holiday, a first step towards achieving the long-standing struggle of making the treaty enforceable in law. In 1973 the Labour government responded by making 6 February a public holiday, a popular decision, although a change of name to New Zealand Day was reversed in 1976. People, it seemed, liked to remember Waitangi.

Protest at Waitangi Day ceremonies began in the 1970s. A succession of Maori groups began to challenge, vocally,

Outside the treaty house grounds, Waitangi, 1982.

Northern elder Simon Snowden speaking at a Waitangi ceremony in 1988. Protests by young Maori have not always been easily accepted by elders who have looked on the treaty as the special work of their ancestors and so still in living memory.

the European record in fulfilling treaty promises; and Pakeha began to search more critically into their history. Historians concluded that previous writers had not fairly evaluated the way the treaty had been made to serve British and settler interests. Many records – official and private, in Maori and in English – had simply been ignored. This information gradually spread widely through the New Zealand public. For most people it was something new and often hard to accept.

Maori leaders speak out

Well-established national Maori organisations also made submissions to the government on the treaty. Such documents were themselves a challenge. Henare Ngata, for instance, concluded one report on the treaty in 1971 by telling the government that 'those who approached it in a positive frame of mind and are prepared to regard it as an obligation of honour will find that the Treaty is well capable of implementation.' He was one of many with similar convictions. But it was still mainly Maori who saw the need for laws to give effect to treaty promises.

The Waitangi Tribunal

In 1975 the third Labour government passed the Treaty of Waitangi Act. Under the act a tribunal was set up comprising three people. Their role was to hear Maori claims and to make recommendations taking into account the 'principles' of the treaty, and for that purpose to determine the treaty's

Protest over government reluctance to heed Maori voices involved Pakeha as well as Maori in the 1970s and 1980s. A Land March in 1975 began at Te Hapua in the far north and ended at Parliament where a petition was presented. Marchers were allowed to cross the Auckland harbour bridge on foot. By the time the march reached the capital it filled Lambton Quay shown here.

Protest at Takaparawha (Bastion Point), 1982. At Bastion Point, Auckland, Maori protest over Ngati Whatua land rights began in the 1970s and continued in the 1980s. The Waitangi tribunal in 1987 suggested a solution for the disputed land which was then worked out by government and Maori.

'meaning and effect'. The tribunal could look at only those claims arising after the 1975 legislation. It was a very limited power indeed and for a time seemed almost useless.

But, under the chairmanship of Chief Judge Edward Durie, the tribunal heard and reported on several major claims: in 1983, a claim by Te Ati Awa over the spoiling of fishing reefs by chemical discharge; in 1984, a claim concerning discharging waste matter into the Kaituna River; and in 1985, a claim over the Manukau Harbour which involved extensive

fishing and usage rights. Much history was painstakingly uncovered by the hearings, but the tribunal had no powers to enforce its recommendations. Yet it had gone quite a way in its task of determining the treaty's meaning and effect.

These claims affected specific tribes and areas. But in late 1985 a claim by the Maori Language Board of Wellington asked the tribunal to recommend that Maori be recognised as an official language throughout the country. Suddenly the public realised that the tribunal's work could affect not only some Maori communities, but all Maori and all Pakeha too. It was a different claim from most and it showed the extent to which Maori leaders wanted treasured aspects – taonga – of being a Maori to be protected under the treaty.

More powers to the tribunal

In 1985 the tribunal's membership was expanded and it was enabled to investigate claims referring back to 1840. A research team works on each claim to arrive at the facts of the case. So, too, do researchers working for the claimant, or for the Crown, or for other interested parties. This work has been expanded even further by another amendment in 1988. Tribunal membership has been further enlarged so that more than one claim can be heard at once.

In February 1984, Kotahitanga was revived in a hikoi (march) to Waitangi in protest against 'celebrating' the day. Waiting for the hikoi were race relations conciliator, Hiwi Tauroa, the governor general, Sir David Beattie, and Northland elder, Sir James Henare. Several national hui to discuss Maori problems followed the hikoi.

At Picton in 1988 land was given back to Maori by minister of lands Peter Tapsell. The land had been taken in 1912 under a public works act and had been used as a rifle range.

Legislation

Unless legislation actually incorporates a reference to the treaty or its principles, the country's law courts have, until recently, decided that they were unable to recognise the treaty. For years this has prevented the Maori people from successfully arguing treaty rights in legal cases. This began to change as the treaty was included in acts. Examples are the State Owned Enterprises Act 1986, the Environment Act 1986, and the Conservation Act 1987.

The principles of the treaty

One clause of the State Owned Enterprises Act notes that 'Nothing in this Act shall permit the Crown to act in a manner that is inconsistent with the principles of the Treaty of Waitangi.' But what those principles are has yet to be agreed upon by government and the Maori people.

In July 1989 the government released a short statement of the principles on which it proposes to act when dealing with issues arising from the treaty. They are:

The government has the right to govern and to make laws.

The iwi have the right to organise as iwi and, under the law, to control the resources they own.

All New Zealanders are equal under the law.

Both the government and the iwi are obliged to accord each other reasonable co-operation on major issues of common concern.

The government is responsible for providing effective processes for the resolution of grievances in the expectation that reconciliation can occur.

Partnership?

The prime minister, David Lange, introduced the principles by saying that the treaty 'has the potential to be our nation's most powerful unifying symbol'. This is true, but many questions must still be worked out. The main one is the relationship of the two peoples to each other, and the relationship of the Maori and the Crown.

The Law Commission, in 1989, had these questions about these relationships:

> How was and is authority to be shared? What things in New Zealand of the year 1989 belong to 'sovereignty' and what to 'rangatiratanga'? What [for example] does it mean in terms both of access to and control over fisheries? And how does it affect the equal rights promised by Article 3?

The commission went on to suggest some of the things that should be taken into account in finding answers.

> The government of a modern State must have the effective power to govern and to make laws. There are such things as overriding national interests. Numerous examples, past and present, prove that this is not incompatible with a considerable degree of autonomy for particular groups. But the dividing line has to be worked out for a particular society at a particular time. It is important to avoid this being done in terms of the values and priorities only of the section holding effective power – in democratic societies like New Zealand, the numerical majority.

Tipene O'Regan speaking at Waitangi commemorations at Okains Bay, Banks Peninsula, 1989. Like many other Maori leaders, he is still engaged in the struggle to secure treaty rights, sometimes in the law courts. A Court of Appeal decision in 1987, in which five judges independently acknowledged Maori rights was encouraging for all leaders.